Honoré Mirabeau

The secret history of the court of Berlin

The character of the present king of Prussia, his ministers, mistresse

Honoré Mirabeau

The secret history of the court of Berlin
The character of the present king of Prussia, his ministers, mistresse

ISBN/EAN: 9783743322264

Manufactured in Europe, USA, Canada, Australia, Japa

Cover: Foto ©ninafisch / pixelio.de

Manufactured and distributed by brebook publishing software (www.brebook.com)

Honoré Mirabeau

The secret history of the court of Berlin

Uniform with the present volume:

"Memoirs of the Empress Josephine." 2 vols.

"Secret Memoirs of the Court of Louis XIV." 1 vol.

"Secret Memoirs of the Royal Family of France." 2 vols.

"The Private Memoirs of Louis XV." 1 vol.

THE
SECRET HISTORY
OF THE
COURT OF BERLIN

Edition strictly limited to 500 copies.

Five extra copies have been printed on Japanese vellum, but are not offered for sale.

FREDERICK WILL.^M II KING of PRUSSIA.

THE
SECRET HISTORY
OF THE
COURT OF BERLIN

OR

THE CHARACTER OF THE KING OF PRUSSIA,
HIS MINISTERS, MISTRESSES, GENERALS,
COURTIERS, FAVOURITES, AND
THE ROYAL FAMILY
OF PRUSSIA

WITH NUMEROUS ANECDOTES OF THE POTENTATES OF EUROPE,
ESPECIALLY OF THE LATE FREDERICK II.

BY

COUNT MIRABEAU

VOLUME I

LONDON
H. S. NICHOLS & CO.
3 SOHO SQUARE AND 62A PICCADILLY W.
MDCCCXCV

Printed and Published by
H. S. NICHOLS AND CO.,
AT 3, SOHO SQUARE, LONDON, W.

PUBLISHERS' NOTE

THIS work, which forms the fifth in our COLLECTION OF COURT MEMOIRS, is of the utmost importance, and the fact that most of the copies have already been subscribed for, even before issue, is sufficient proof of the eagerness with which it is awaited, and of the great interest it has already aroused.

The French edition was condemned by the laws in France, and had its funeral oration pronounced by M. Seguier, and was then publicly burnt by the common hangman.

In the original edition, issued in England in 1789, all the names were left blank. We have filled in these names in almost every instance; but in cases where they still are left blank, they are so in both the French and English editions.

With regard to the omitted passages, indicated by asterisks, these existed only in Mirabeau's original MS., and have never been printed, and as, unfortunately, the MS. was burnt, they never can be printed.

The sixth work in this Collection, which will be issued during next month, will be "The Secret History of the Court and Cabinet of St. Cloud," in a series of letters from a Gentleman in Paris to a Nobleman in London, written during the months of August, September, and October, 1805.

LONDON, 5th *April*, 1895.

EDITOR'S PREFACE

To "The Secret History of the Court of Berlin," and to the "Key" of that History.

MIRABEAU, exiled to Prussia on a secret mission, has left behind him, in the following work, a curious account of his sojourn at the Court of Frederick the Great. It is generally supposed that these letters were addressed to Calonne.

The last moments of Frederick are therein depicted in a vivid and lifelike manner, and every portrait that Mirabeau essayed to paint bears the mark of a master's hand. However, Frederick dies, and the writer has no longer anything but low intrigues to depict, as he is now surrounded only by little men and little interests.

If he is reproached with including in this work several scandalous revelations, it must be remembered that "The Secret History" was never intended to see the light of day, and that it was quite contrary to the author's wishes that it was published. It was also in direct opposition to his wishes that the "*Lettres à Sophie*," and others of his productions, were issued.

The manuscript of "The Secret History" was stolen, sold to Malassis, a printer of Alençon, and published by him as a work by an unknown traveller who had died about a year previously in a village in Germany. Twenty thousand copies of the book were speedily disposed of.

The original manuscript, in Mirabeau's handwriting, remained in the printer's possession, and great care was taken that, in every edition issued by him, all the names and certain passages were suppressed and indicated by asterisks only. Unfortunately, the manuscript was subsequently burnt. M. Dubois-du-Desert, who had the privilege of inspecting this manuscript before its destruction, has communicated to us all the names, of which he had taken a note. This it is that is known as the "Key" to "The Secret History." A very small number of the names have been lost, and it is impossible for us, after this long interval, to repair these omissions.

The following are some appropriate reflections included in the Preface, written by M. Brissot-Thivars, for the edition of 1821:—

"The ministerial modesty, which so easily reconciled itself to the secret picture of the licentiousness of a neighbouring Court, grew much alarmed at the prospect of a similar picture of their own Court being exhibited to the public gaze. The Government received orders to confiscate the book and to prosecute the author, who had disappeared under an anonymous name. Meanwhile the public were much rejoiced at the ill-humour displayed by the Court.

"The *États-Généraux* were convoked, the nobility repulsed Mirabeau, the Commons welcomed him with open arms, and the privileged classes heaped insults and abuse upon the head of the author of 'The Secret History.'"

Amongst the most noticeable pamphlets issued at this period was one entitled "*L'Examen politique et critique de l'Histoire secrète de la Cour de Berlin,*" par Frédéric, Baron de Trenck.[1]

"The Baron de Trenck was a Prussian, and had, therefore, some right to enter the lists. It was also to his interest to do so, as for some time he had been in bad odour with his Government, and he was only too rejoiced to purchase his pardon by breaking a lance in honour of his country.

"Mirabeau pretends that the Prussians are a dull people. The Baron de Trenck admits that this is the case; but, he adds, they are so systematically.

"Mirabeau hints that the two sons of Prince Ferdinand are really the sons of the Comte de Schmettau. The Baron de Trenck replies that he has closely examined the children of Princess Ferdinand. 'They are,' he says, 'destined to occupy glorious positions in the House of Brandenburg. I would never guarantee,' he adds, 'the birth of any man; all that I can certify is that he is the son of a man. It is to be hoped that, in certain European royal families, they will act as they do in England towards the racehorses. It is unnecessary and absurd to try and discover who are the fathers of the kings who rule

---

[1] "Political and Critical Examination of the Secret History of the Court of Berlin," by Frédéric, Baron de Trenck. A thick 8vo volume. The Baron de Trenck was known by his misfortunes and by his sundry writings.

over us. It is often much better that they owe their existence to wise and vigorous plebeians than to a self-styled "noble" race, which is in no way superior to others, save by an opinion based upon absurd prejudices. I heartily congratulate Prince Ferdinand on being the head of so interesting a family.'

"Mirabeau, having related some amorous scenes of Frederick William, the Baron gravely examines the two following questions:—

"1. Is it true that the King of Prussia is fond of women? Nobody doubts it.

"2. Is this a crime in a king? William, in love, is capable of a tender attachment. He understands how to value his mistress. Refined and sensitive, it is by the personal interest that he inspires, that he endeavours to find favour in the eyes of the woman he loves. He puts aside all rank and power. It is solely for himself that he would win the lady's affection. Mademoiselle de Voss resisted his wooing during twenty months. The tardy gratification of his desires did not cool his passion. In the present condition of Prussia, the King may prefer the myrtles of Cupid to the laurels of Mars.

"Did the reputation of Baron de Trenck re-establish Frederick William and the Prince Ferdinand—the one in his paternal rights, and the other in the respect and veneration which a virtuous monarch has the right to expect from his subjects? We do not think it did. It appears to us, on the contrary, that it will remain proved that Mirabeau had correctly observed, and that he stated the truth, since his adversary is reduced to representing concubinage and adultery as the accustomed pastime of the nobility and as the legitimate resource of a monarch. Mirabeau's statements, therefore, must have been based largely on facts, since there did not exist any other means of extenuating the scandal.

"In the absence of logic and reason, Baron de Trenck had recourse to abuse of Mirabeau, whom he vilified as an impostor and a spy. Such insults, however, prove nothing; and, even at the present time, there are those who firmly believe in the truth of Mirabeau's assertions.[1]

"At the date of the publication of 'The Secret History,' time had strongly confirmed nearly all of Mirabeau's predictions—the invasion of Holland, the ridiculous combinations of the French Cabinet, &c., at the present day—after a lapse of thirty years. Some personages who are still living are attacked; for instance, he says, on page 176, 'The Duke of York arrived here this evening. This Duke is a great sportsman, fond of laughter, but without grace, deportment, or politeness; and, judging from external appearances, he possesses many of the moral and physical features of the Duc de Luynes. I do not think that there is any question of his marriage with Princess Caroline of Brunswick, who is very amiable, intellectual, handsome, and vivacious.'"

---

[1] In all matters apart from the Prussian monarchy, or ministry, and any facts relating to either, Baron de Trenck renders full justice to Mirabeau; he even admits the accuracy of Mirabeau's estimates of political affairs, and of his profound knowledge of the actual state of Europe.

The Princess Caroline, who was married in 1759 to the Prince of Wales, was divorced after he had become King of England.

"It must be admitted, however, that Mirabeau was sometimes mistaken in his judgments. He judged mankind; and, for good or for evil, the human species is subject to variations. Time and education modify the character, and alter the inclinations. The horoscope that Mirabeau cast of the Prince Royal of Prussia, the present reigning monarch, was it realized? Did that Prince resuscitate the great Frederick?"

Mirabeau recommends l'Abbé de Périgord to M. de Calonne. "L'Abbé de Périgord," he says, "combines a talent of a rare order and great experience with a profound circumspection and an unfailing secrecy. It would be impossible for you to choose a man who is more anxious to do good, and who would be more eager to show his gratitude." Prince Talleyrand, before the Revolution, bore the name of *l'Abbé de Périgord*.

Amongst the curious facts relating to this work, we should not omit to give a copy of the Decree ordering it to be burnt. We reproduce this document as an example of the jurisprudence of the period.

"Decree of the Court of Parliament, the Chambers assembled, the Peers being present, condemning a printed book entitled: '*The Secret History of the Court of Berlin; or, the Correspondence of a French Traveller*" (Count Mirabeau, *Député de la Sénéchaussée d'Aix aux États-Généraux*), to be torn and burnt by the Public Executioner."

Extract from the Parliamentary Register of the 10th of February, 1789.

"This day the Court, the Chambers assembled, the Peers being present, and the King's representatives being admitted, M. Antoine-Louis Seguier, Advocate to the King, opened the proceedings in the following words:

"'Gentlemen,—Justly indignant at the impression produced by a libel as surprising as it is atrocious, the King, in placing in our hands the two printed works which we have brought before you, relies upon the vigilance of the Ministry to denounce and condemn them.

"'This libel, which has spread itself throughout the Capital, has already caused the greatest sensation. It has been received with a cry of indignation, the public verdict has been given, and this work of darkness has already been stamped with the seal of universal reprobation.

"'It is within the rights of Justice to proscribe, with the strongest qualifications, a correspondence which the author seeks to disown by announcing it as the secret agent of a Minister who wishes to remain unknown. In denouncing this clandestine work, therefore, we propose to proceed against both the author and the printer, if it is possible to discover them.

"'You will doubtless feel some surprise that our Ministry, so long a dumb recipient of the complaints addressed to it by all the Orders of the State, was not to be awakened out of its voluntary inaction, excepting by the command of the King himself. But at this critical moment, when every day sees some fresh production, alternately extravagant and wise, violent and moderate, circumspect and licentious, dictated by party spirit and inspired by patriotism; in this universal madness, when the indefinite liberty of the Press distributes with equal profusion the fruits of knowledge, of ignorance, and of frenzy; in this total inversion of principles, it required nothing less than an order emanating from the Throne to decide us to fulfil those functions which would be indispensable under all other circumstances, but which it seemed to us prudent to suspend, in the midst of the fanaticism of opinions. There are moments when, by a kind of public discretion, or decency, the magistrate should not consult the oracle of the Law.

"'There is no need for dissimulation on our part, and we regard with an unfeeling eye the product of resentment and vengeance. The past is a guarantee for the future. We have no fear in making this avowal in the presence of magistrates who, whilst demanding the legitimate liberty of the Press, are very far from countenancing the publication of the deluge of anonymous sheets, and the seditious and scandalous pamphlets, with which France is inundated. Tolerance degenerates into abuse, impunity encourages licence, and licence has reached its last stage. Nothing is respected; rank, position, services rendered are forgotten; the nobles, and even crowned heads themselves, become objects of derision and satire. The evil is so widespread that one fears to augment the epidemic in attempting to stay its progress.

"'The slightest prohibition of a work is sufficient to make the author celebrated, to accelerate its sale, at double the original price, and to give a wider publicity to imposture and calumny.

"'The work which we are now denouncing was not written with the intention of still further fertilizing the germs of discord which are already too much scattered throughout the Kingdom, but it is of a nature likely to influence the reception, and the mode of existence, of the French nobility at foreign Courts; and far from confirming the high opinion which it has always gained for its generosity, far from being characterized by that frank and loyal spirit of ancient chivalry, which led it on to honour and glory, this vile and infamous production cannot but inspire the strongest prejudice against a people at once polite, natural, complaisant, and quick to familiarize itself wherever it finds an opportunity of displaying its wit, or of captivating hearts by the charm of that sociability which distinguishes it from the other European nations.

"'This work, in two volumes, is entitled: "*The Secret History of the Court of Berlin; or, Correspondence of a French Traveller, from the month of July*, 1786, *until the 19th January*, 1787. *Posthumous work*, 1789"; without the names of either author or printer, nor the place where printed.

"'This title would seem to indicate that the author was no longer in existence, and that the work was therefore published without his knowledge or consent; but supposing, as the title-page states, that the Secret History is the result of observations made by a writer who had ceased to exist, if it has taken two entire years to print and distribute a work of this nature, is it not obvious that the publisher is even more culpable than the author, since he has given publicity to a correspondence written under the seal of confidence, and which, therefore, was never intended to become a means of defamation, or to supply food for the scandal-mongers?

"'The period at which this Secret History commences will be for ever memorable in the annals of Germany. The short space of time which it includes was full of events likely to affect the policy of many a monarchy. Frederick II., whose name alone was sufficient to preserve that balance of power which assured to Europe general peace and happiness, Frederick still reigned; but this prince was fast declining, and his power and fame, which did not abandon him during life, seemed to await him even at the tomb.

"'It was at this moment that the self-styled "*Voyageur français*" endeavoured to ingratiate himself with the greatest personages of the State, in order to gather any stray scraps of conversation, and to endeavour, in the midst of the trouble and commotion caused by the unforeseen changes of a new ruler, to surprise ministerial secrets, to detect the aims and ambitions of the nobles, to expose the intrigues of courtesans, and to fathom the plots of the Court.

"'If one is to believe this disguised observer, his ability surmounts all obstacles. He is at once welcomed, and, far from being suspected, he seems to have obtained almost general confidence. Princes treat him with kindness; the ministers put him in possession of State secrets; the nobles admit him into their society; the political veil is rent asunder for his benefit; Frederick dies, Frederick William succeeds him; the army has not yet taken the oath of allegiance, and yet this attentive politician is aware of the spirit, the character, and the resources of those in authority. The plan of administration is no longer a mystery, and even the King himself, who suspects his mission, does not take offence at his assiduity or his *liaisons*.

"'After having explained the system upon which the correspondence would be based: after having explained the sources from which he proposes to draw his information; in fact, after having exposed his relations and his intimacy with the principal members of the Royal Family, the first object with which the author has thought it his duty to concern himself, is the panegyric on the king which Prussia has just lost. He eulogizes that great man, and he is nearly the only person of whom he speaks highly, or even of whom he does not speak ill, in a Secret History, which has no other authenticity than that of the observations, estimates, and the combinations, true or false, of a writer who possessed neither title nor qualification.

"'And how was it that he did not render to Frederick II. the justice that was his due? Worthy of the admiration of his century, our soldiers were sent to be instructed in his schools, to study his manœuvres and his evolutions, and, above all, his military discipline, in the hope of transferring to France some portion of that genius which had founded a new school of tactics, and which had, in some sort, revolutionized the art of war. Amongst the homage which truth sometimes forces from this mysterious correspondent, one discovers reproaches against the memory of the greatest man in Europe; but, notwithstanding this critical observer and his remarks, his reflections and his criticisms, Frederick, the friend of science and the protector of literature, legislator and philosopher, profound politician and indefatigable warrior, combined in his person, and displayed on his throne, all the gifts of a hero and a king. His name, even before his death, was inscribed in the temple of Immortality.

"'Why did not the author of this correspondence show the same respect for a Prince of the same blood, animated by the same spirit, and endowed with the same talents? Did not Prince Henry prove himself to be a general worthy of commanding his august brother, to second his views, and to execute his projects? Frederick himself, on learning of his success, could not suppress a feeling of rivalry. The greatest generals and the most famous captains are sometimes at fault; the ablest have their reverses. Alone exempt from the common destiny of mankind, fortune seems, in his case, to have renounced its natural inconsistency, or rather, the experience of Prince Henry enabled him to control the caprices of fortune, and to fix the victory under his standard. Could we but examine here the witnesses of his brave deeds, the companions of his glory, the only true judges of his merit, they would say, with one voice, that, gentle and affable in the every-day affairs of life, intrepid and at ease in action, humane and compassionate after the combat, by a most happy accord of the most eminent qualities, he combined the activity of Hannibal, the prudence of Fabius, and the wisdom of Scipio.

"'But is it necessary for us to call witnesses to prove the bravery and genius of a Prince whose name is revered by both officers and soldiers? It is for the French Army to avenge the insults. A magistrate, a friend of peace, is not the proper man to pronounce his eulogy; and the Minister of Justice would hardly dare to add his voice to the general acclamations of this celebrated Prince.

"'One is tempted to believe that, from the midst of his "nebulous position," the author has taken upon himself to open the floodgates of his malice and animosity on all those whose positions and characters are above suspicion, and who are worthy of his respect. It is not enough to have showered invectives on the uncle of the new King, the King himself, his august family, the Princesses of the blood, and the Ministry; in fact, the whole Court is treated with such a criminal indecency, that we should blush to repeat the infamous expressions of which the author has made use.

"'His "amphibious existence" enables him sometimes to wander from his native land; his imagination transports him to far distant countries, to Austria, to Poland, and to the northernmost lands; and it is always with the same culpable purpose of collecting fresh horrors, of filling his correspondence with untruthful statements, and to circulate with his discoveries the blackest calumnies.

"'What opinion can one form of this Secret History, which is even more abominable than that of the historian Procopius, who, when criticizing an emperor, did at least refer to his merits as well as his demerits? It presents us with nothing but a collection of shameful impostures, highly improbable and easily invented, more for the purpose of gratifying the mania of the author, than for attracting the curiosity of the reader in search of knowledge.

"'It is a collection of portraits in which the artist's imagination is largely predominant. His hand has mixed the colours with the bitter spleen with which his brush was already filled; and if we are told that he painted his subjects as they appeared to him, it must be remembered that his prejudiced eye enveloped them in that shade in which he was himself obscured.

"'It is an assemblage of reflections based indiscriminately upon malicious conversations, upon lying reports, upon fictitious secrets, and upon facts which have since been proved untrue. All these have been written down without thought or hesitation, and the author has no fear in asserting that they are veritable facts, because it was the only return he could make for the treatment he received, of the mediocrity of which he is constantly complaining.

"'It is most unfortunate to possess great talent when one has not sufficient force of character to apply it to good purposes. If the corruption of the soul stifle the sentiment of honour and the cry of conscience, genius is a disastrous gift from Nature. What are we to think of a writer who voluntarily adopts the rôle of anonymous accuser; who settles himself in a foreign Court with that frankness, that ease, that amenity, which leads to the forming of liaisons; and who, ere long, abusing the sentiments which he had inspired, dares to reveal particulars which he has learnt in the most intimate confidence; who dares to slander all those who have received him with kindness, dares to make insinuations and suggestions concerning them which are entirely unjustifiable; and who even carries his audacity to the length of insulting, with a brutal cynicism, those whose station is so greatly above that of this "*agent subalterne*" (for so he styles himself) that it is difficult to place any confidence in his assertions; because, if they were true, his relations with people of rank must have been most intimate—in fact, they must have treated him as an equal. Again, what man would wish to expose himself before his equal? The noble may lay aside their rank in their own households; it is frequently necessary for them to do so. But a king, or a prince, or a man of dignity, always knows how to respect himself before a stranger; should any familiarities or confidences be accorded to him, it is done with suspicion and is but temporary.

"'What must have been the result, therefore, when this stranger himself admits that he is regarded as a spy? And if he is suspected of wishing to find out the secrets of the Government, would not a wise circumspection suggest the advisability of deceiving him by making a pretence of that confidence which he is so eager to abuse?

"'Let us suppose, nevertheless, that the author,

deceived by false reports or by feigned contrivances, believed that he was really a witness of all that he inserted in his correspondence: the entire work would still be a violation of the Law of Nations, an abuse of hospitality, an infamy the more unpardonable in that familiarity was with him but the cloak of perfidiousness, and that the closest friendship became the instrument of treachery.

"'These reflections lead necessarily to the pronouncement of judgment both upon the author of this pretended posthumous work and upon the work itself. And, in the first place, it is by simple and by sure rules that the author may be judged without error.

"'Has he placed himself beyond the laws of honour and probity? Has he gone beyond the bounds of decency? Has he so far forgotten himself as to violate public morality? Has he been wanting in that respect of which the French are ever ready to accord the most touching proofs to their King — respect impelled as much by love as by duty, but respect that every Frenchman owes to other nations, whether they are friends or enemies of France; which every man owes to other men, and which everyone owes to himself? This writer has an unruly spirit. His natural perversity makes him rash, violent, and passionate; and after having broken down all the barriers that prudence opposes to his licence, he only brings trouble and remorse into the hearts of those who are unfortunate enough to allow themselves to be entrapped by his fables, his lies and his calumnies.

"'We are, nevertheless, bound to admit that if

this unknown author only fulfilled the particular mission which he pretends to have received; if the letters which compose this Secret History were written by him only to be sent direct to their destination; if he made no copies of them; if it was not by his act that they were made public; in fact, if he is entirely innocent of the printing of this work, however ignominious may be the obscure person who played this part, it is for him alone to reproach himself with his baseness and crime, and justice cannot hold as a crime the publication of his correspondence. The publisher only merits prosecution, and the printer, equally guilty, should share the punishment of an offence which is as contrary to public honesty as it is to the Law of Nations.

"'With regard to the work itself, it is difficult to consider this "*correspondence*" otherwise than as a defamatory libel worthy of all the rigour of the law. By a species of fatality, writings of this nature generally excite the curiosity; the more they are vicious, the more they are sought after. The human heart permits itself to be so easily attracted towards that which is evil. In censuring the writer, one gives publicity to his libels. The malicious smile, the honest man contents himself with a sigh, and the defamation remains unpunished; whereas general indignation should denounce and prosecute the slanderer. "*The Secret History of the Court of Berlin*" has not received the same indulgent treatment. Public opinion was shocked, and it measured the insult, not by the man who uttered it, but by the elevated position of those against whom it was directed. The disparity of rank seemed to add to the gravity of the outrage. The libel was regarded as sufficient to excite the indignation of all the Powers, should the law not hasten to proscribe the work.

"'It is by the King's command that we have denounced this fictitious correspondence; it is in his name that we demand its condemnation; and after having consigned it to the flames, we call upon the ministry to employ every effort for the discovery of the author, publisher, and printer.

"'This, then, is the conclusion of our indictment, which we place before the Court, together with the two volumes referred to, of which the following is a faithful description:—

"'A printed work, in two volumes, entitled: "*The Secret History of the Court of Berlin; or, Correspondence of a French Traveller, from the month of July,* 1786, *until* 19*th January,* 1787. *A posthumous work,* 1789"; without names of either the author or printer, containing— Vol. i., 318 pages; vol. ii., 376 pages.'

[*Conclusion of the indictment of the Procureur-général of the King. Follows the decision of the Court.*]

"The Court orders that the two volumes be destroyed and burnt in the court-yard of the palace, at the foot of the grand staircase, by the public executioner, the Court being of the opinion that the volumes contain defamatory and slanderous libels, which are contrary to the respect due to other Powers, and in opposition to our laws and those of other nations. The Court calls upon all those who possess copies of this work to deliver them up to the clerk of this Court in order that they may be destroyed. It also strictly prohibits all printers and booksellers from printing or selling copies of this work, and all *colporteurs* and distributors from hawking or distributing it, under penalty of prosecution and punishment with such rigour as the law may permit. And the Court further ordains that, at the request of the *Procureur-général* of the King, information may be heard against the author, printer, and publisher, before the *Conseilleur-rapporteur* that the Court may appoint, for the witnesses at Paris ; and before the *Lieutenant-criminel des bailliages et sénéchaussées du ressort,* for such witnesses as may reside in the provinces, having regard to the printing and distributing of this work. The Court ordains that the present decree be printed and posted up in all public places, and that copies may be sent to all *bailliages et sénéchaussées du ressort,* for a similar purpose. The Court enjoins upon the deputies of the *Procureur-général du roi* to give this matter their attention, and to report to the Court within a month from this date. Given in Parliament, fully assembled, the Peers being present, the tenth day of February, the year Seventeen hundred and eighty-nine.

"(Verified)   CLUTTON.
"(Signed)   ISABEAU.

" And the same date (10th February, 1789), at the rising of the Court, the aforesaid work, entitled '*The Secret History of the Court of Berlin ; or, Correspondence of a French Traveller,*' was destroyed and burnt by the public executioner, at the foot of the grand staircase in the Palace, in the presence of me, Dagobert-Étienne Isabeau, esquire, one of the clerks of the *Grande Chambre*, assisted by two ushers of the Court.

"(Signed)   Isabeau."

At the end of the Secret History will be found a letter addressed by Mirabeau to Frederick William II., on the day of his ascension to the Throne. He was the nephew of the great Frederick, and the father of the present King.

This Prince is not much known as a soldier, his only experience in the art of warfare being during the invasion of Champagne in 1792. He received Mirabeau's letter with kindness, but he did not foresee the destiny which the "*Voyageur français*" had traced for him.

C. Y.

THE SECRET HISTORY OF THE COURT OF BERLIN

LETTER I[1]

July 5th, 1786.

SIR,—I have the honour to write to you by the first post, to inform you that the Berlin mail, for which I waited before I would enter my carriage, has brought me no letter. It is possible, but not probable, that the letter of my correspondent has been sent too late for the post. It is also possible,

---

[1] This letter is evidently addressed to a minister, who had given the traveller some secret commission to execute. It seems evident to us that this minister was M. de Calonne; and the following letter is extremely curious, as it leads to prove that, from the beginning of the year 1786, M. de Calonne was determined on the assembly of the Notables; whom he convoked and directed, in 1787, with so much perilous and fatal precipitation.

and very likely, nay, if the Count de Vergennes has received no intelligence it is almost certain, that the great event either approaches or is past; for I hold it as infallible, that when death becomes inevitable the couriers will be stopped. This, sir, deeply engages my attention, and I shall hasten with all expedition to Brunswick, where I shall gain certain information;—there I shall remain several days if the King is living.

I have at present only to add, I shall think no labour, time or trouble too great if I can but serve you, sir, and the cause of the public.

    ✧   ✧   ✧   ✧

I shall not repeat any of our conversations, but shall take the liberty to offer you my advice, solely founded on my personal attachment; of which you cannot doubt, since, independent of that amiable seduction which you exercise with power so irresistible, our interests are the same. The torrent of your affairs, the activity of cabals, the efforts of every kind which you so prodigally are obliged to make, render it impossible that you should yourself class and arrange the grand projects which your genius has brought to maturity, and which are ready to bud and bloom. You have testified some regret that I, for the present, declined performing this office for you. Permit me therefore, sir, to name a person who is in every respect worthy of this mark of your confidence.

The Abbé de Périgord, to consummate and practical abilities, joins profound circumspection and inviolable secrecy. You never can select a man more to be depended upon; or one who will with more fervent piety bow before the shrine of gratitude and friendship; who will be more anxiously active in good, less covetous of others fame, or one with superior conviction that fame is justly due to him, only, who has the power to conceive and the fortitude to execute.

He possesses another advantage. His ascendancy over Panchand represses the defects of the latter, which have been so described to you as to inspire fears, and sets all his great qualities and uncommon talents, which daily become more necessary to you, in action. There is no man who can guide and rule Mr. Panchand like the Abbé de Périgord, who will momentarily become more valuable to you the better to effect a grand money measure, without which no other measures can be effected. You may confide that delicate business to the Abbé de Périgord, which, especially in the present moment, ought not to be trusted to clerks. The noble, the enlightened, the civic project of drawing inferences from the numerous false statements that infest the accounts of ministers (and which, being compared to the true statements, caused, or rather obliged, the King to determine that decisive measures should give France a national credit, and consequently a legal constitution) cannot be better realized than by the joint labours of these two persons. One of them has long been devoted to you; and the other will be, whenever any single act of benevolence shall excite his emulation. Condescend to believe, sir, that you cannot act more to your own interest.

I was desirous of writing thus to-night, because it would neither be delicate nor decent for the person interested to read what I have written; and this letter is the last you will receive, that must not pass through the hands of a third person. My attachment, sir, to you, and your fame, induces me to hope you will place some confidence in this counsel, if I may so venture to call it; and that it will not be ranked among the least of the proofs of the most devoted respect with which I am, &c.

LETTER II

Brunswick, July 12th, 1786.

THAT the King is very ill is very certain; but he is not at the point of death. Zimmermann, the famous Hanoverian physician, whom he sent for, has declared that, if he would be careful, he might still live; but he is incorrigible on the article of abstinence. He still mounts his horse, and he even trotted fifty paces, some days since, with a man on each side of him; but it is nevertheless true that he has the dropsy; and, in reality, he has not been any better since my departure.

I shall not see the reigning Duke of Brunswick before this evening: he is in the country. He has powerfully supported the election which the chapters of Hildesheim and Paderborn have lately made of a coadjutor. M. Furstemberg has been elected. Vienna caballed exceedingly in favour of the Arch-Duke Maximilian. It appears that the Duke wishes to promote peace, since he endeavours, by every means, to strengthen the Germanic confederation, which certainly has that only for its end, though the means may give room for reflection. I have my reasons for being of that opinion, which I shall explain on some other occasion. To-day I am at the mercy of the courier.

Parties are very busy at Berlin; especially that of Prince Henry, who is eternally eager, without well knowing what he wishes. But all is silence in the King's presence; he still is King, and so will remain to the last moment.

* *

As the immediate death of the King is not expected, I shall continue at Brunswick some days, in order to prepare him for my return (much more premature than I had announced) and that I may more nearly study the Duke.

The coinage continues to be an object of contention, and exaggerated discredit. I think it would be of use to publish apologetic reasons concerning the gold coin, confessing its too high rate; (for wherefore deny that which is demonstrated?) and justificatory proofs, relative to the silver, the crowns of sixty-nine, and those since 1784, still remaining prohibited.

You no doubt know that the Duke, Louis of Brunswick,[1] has quitted Aix-la-Chapelle, and is retired to Eisenach. The troubles of that petty republic may perhaps explain his retreat; but these do not seem to me sufficient motives for his new abode, and for this single reason, that the Duchess of Weymar is his niece.

---

[1] Not the reigning Duke of Brunswick, just before mentioned, but his uncle, the late prime minister of the Stadtholder; or rather the late effective regent of the United Provinces.

LETTER III

July 14th, 1786.

I DINED and supped yesterday with the Duke. When we rose from table, after dinner, he took me aside to the window, where we conversed for about two hours, with much reserve at first, on his part, afterward with more openness, and at last with an evident desire to be thought sincere.

An expression of esteem for the Count de Vergennes, and fear for his approaching retreat, gave occasion to this private conversation. The expression alluded to was immediately followed by the question (which was asked in a tone of affected indifference, and betrayed a very strong degree of curiosity)—" No doubt M. de Breteuil will be his successor?" The Duchess was of our party. I answered, lowering my voice, but articulating with great firmness—" I hope and believe not."—It was after I had said this that he led me to the window, at the far end of the apartment. He presently began to converse, with all the energy of which his slowness and native dignity admit, of the inquietude which the Germanic body could not avoid feeling, should M. de Breteuil, who was at the head of the Austrian party, and who has long been a servant and friend of the cabinet of Vienna, succeed to the place of first minister.

I replied (speaking of the Count de Vergennes with every respect, and of the generous and pacific intentions of the King with great confidence) that, should the Count de Vergennes retire, it would probably be of his own free will; and that no one would have greater influence than himself in the choice of his successor; that consequently, whether he remained in office or went out, the first minister would not be of the Austrian party; and, though most assuredly the probity of the King, and the moral of his politics, would continue to render the connections between the Courts of Vienna and Versailles respected, as they would all others, yet, that the interest of Europe, and of France in particular, was so intimately united to the continuance of peace, that these connections, far from inciting war, could but contribute to render peace durable;

that France was suifficently puissant, from innate strength and from the state of her affairs, honourably to own that she dreaded war, which she would take every care to shun; that I did not think sudden war probable, especially when, studying the administration of the Duke of Brunswick, I perceived that he had performed his duties, of prince and father, with so much assiduity and success; that, however natural it might be for man to seek that career, in which he was indubitably the first, I could not believe he (the Duke) would sacrifice to the desire of military renown, so much of which he had already acquired, his favourite work, his real enjoyments, and the inheritance of his children; that all circumstances called him to supreme influence over the affairs of Prussia, after the death of the great King, and that, Prussia being at this time the pivot on which continental war or peace were balanced, he (the Duke of Brunswick) would almost singly decide which was to ensue; that he had formerly sufficiently shone the hero of war, and that I was convinced he would hereafter remain the angel of peace.

He then forcibly denied ever having been fond of war; even at the time when he had been most fortunate. He shewed, independent of his principles, how ardently his family and personal interest would induce him to beware of war.—" And if it were necessary," added he, "in an affair so important, to consult nothing further than the despicable gratification of self-love, do I not know how much war is the sport of chance? I have formerly not been unfortunate. I might hereafter be a better general, and yet might not have the same success. No prudent man, especially one who is advanced in life, will risk his reputation in so hazardous a pursuit, if it may be avoided."

This part of his discourse, which was long, animated, energetic, and evidently sincere, was preceded by a phrase of etiquette and remonstrance, in which he assured me that he never should possess, and was far from desiring to possess, any influence in Prussia. To this phrase I reverted; and, by a rapid sketch, proving to him that I was well acquainted with Berlin, the principal actors there, and the present state of men and things, I demonstrated (which he most certainly knows better than I do) that his interest, the interest of his house, of Germany and of Europe, made it a duty in him to take the helm of state in Prussia; to preserve that kingdom from * the hurricane most fatal to states, the strength of which principally depends upon opinion. I mean from petty intrigues, petty passions, and want of stability and consistency of system. "Your personal dignity," added I, "which is truly immense, and a thousand times more elevated than your rank, however eminent that may be, no doubt forbids you to tender your services; but it is your duty, I will not say not to refuse, no, I repeat, it is your duty to take measures, and employ all your abilities, all your powers, to gain an ascendancy over the successor, and to seize the direction of affairs."

This mode of treatment greatly developed the man. He spoke with truth, and consequently with a degree of confidence, of Berlin. He told me Count Hertzberg had not let him remain ignorant of our intimacy: he depicted many of the persons who have influence, such as I know them to be. I clearly saw that there was a coolness, founded on some unknown subject, between him and the Prince of Prussia[1]; that he (the Duke of Brunswick) neither loved nor esteemed Prince Henry; and that his (the Duke's) party was as powerfully formed' as it could be, in a country hitherto little in the habit of cabal, but which, perhaps, will presently be initiated. I purposely assumed much faith in the warlike dispositions of the cabinet of Berlin. The Duke gave good proofs that, independent of the Heir Apparent, who, though personally brave, was not warlike, as well because of his manners and habits as of his prodigious stature, that it would be madness to begin; that the moment of acquisition by arms, which, perhaps, still was necessary to Prussia, was not yet come; and that it was necessary to consolidate, &c., &c. All this was very serious, very sensible, and very circumstantial.

The Oriental system, Russia, Poland, Courland, all passed in review.

They still have their fears concerning the

---

[1] The Heir Apparent.

Oriental system; that is to say, concerning the part that we might take. They seem to believe that Russia will never powerfully second the Emperor, except in support of the Oriental system, and whatever may contribute to its success. Poland is to reconstruct. We remitted speaking of it, as well as of Courland. Suddenly, and by a very abrupt transition—(It seems to me he employs transitions to surprise the secrets of those with whom he converses, and on whom he earnestly fixes his eyes while he listens)—he asked what I meant to do at Berlin.—"Complete my knowledge of the North," answered I, "which I have had little opportunity of studying, except at that city; since Vienna and Petersburg are to me forbidden places. And who knows? We always presume on our own powers. It may be hoped that, the subject being so grand, the soul may elevate the genius. I, perhaps, shall dare to snatch the portrait of Cæsar from the daubers who are so eager to besmear."—This answer seemed satisfactory. I found it easy to interlard my discourse with agreeable compliments. I told him he had rather conquered than vanquished us;

that we regarded the fate of Germany as resting on his shoulders, &c., &c.; and that therefore the design of writing the most brilliant period of the history of the age in which I lived had placed me, even before I was acquainted with him, in the rank of one of his most ardent admirers. I know not whether he did or did not believe that I solely occupied myself with literature; but the supposition that I shall write history will perhaps render him more accessible to me, and acquire me more of his confidence; for he appears to possess the love, and even the jealousy, of fame to the utmost degree.

I am pressed by the courier because, not having quitted the Court all yesterday, I could not write before this morning; and the courier departs at eleven o'clock. Writing in cypher is very tedious; I therefore omit a thousand particulars which lead me to believe—

1. That the English will not, by any means, be so quickly successful in their artifices in the North as might be feared; if the Court of Berlin may at all depend on the Court of Versailles.

2. That it is time to speak a little more

openly to the former; and not to confound mystery and secrecy, finesse and prudence, ambiguity and policy.

3. That the Duke of Brunswick, whom I believe to be by much the most able Prince of Germany, is sincerely desirous of peace; and that he will inspire the Cabinet of Berlin with the same sentiments, if but the least restraint be laid on the Emperor; who, said he to me, has spoken in outrageous terms, in the presence of seven or eight witnesses beside myself, of the Prince of Prussia.

4. That the intention of the Duke is to govern Prussia, and to obtain great confidence and superior influence in Europe; that he would dread lest these would not be augmented by war, which he is convinced ought to be avoided, at Berlin; and that war is not really to be feared, except as far as France shall encourage the Emperor, who without us will not be anything.

I have not time to-day to give more than a sketch of the Duke such as he appears to me, who certainly will not be thought a common man even among men of merit. His person bespeaks depth and penetration, a desire to please tempered by fortitude, nay by severity. He is polite to affectation; speaks with precision, and with a degree of elegance; but he is somewhat too careful to speak thus, and the proper word sometimes escapes him. He understands the art of listening, and of interrogating according to the very spirit of reply. Praise, gracefully embellished and artfully concealed, he finds agreeable. He is prodigiously laborious, well-informed, and perspicuous. However able his first minister Feronce may be, the Duke superintends all affairs, and generally decides for himself. His correspondence is immense, for which he can only be indebted to his personal consideration; because he cannot be sufficiently wealthy to keep so many correspondents in pay; and few great Courts are so well informed as he is. All his affairs are in excellent order. He became the reigning Duke of Brunswick in 1780, and found his principality loaded with debts, to the amount of forty millions of livres: his administration has been such that, with a revenue of about one hundred thousand pounds sterling, and a sinking fund in which he has deposited the savings of the English subsidies, he will, in 1790, not only have perfectly liquidated the debts of the sovereignty, but, also, those of the state. His country is as free as it can be; and is happy and contented, except that the trading class regret the prodigality of his father. Not that the reigning Duke is less sensible to elegant pleasures than another; but, severely observant of decency, and religiously faithful to his duty as a Prince, he has perceived that economy was his only resource. His mistress, Madam Hartfeld, is the most reasonable woman at Court: and so proper is this attachment that, having a short time since discovered an inclination for another woman, the Duchess leagued with Madam Hartfeld to keep her at a distance. Truly an Alcibiades, he delights in the pleasures and the graces; but these never subtract anything from his labours or his duties, not even those of prudence. When he is to act as a Prussian general, no one is so early, so active, so minute as himself. It is a mark of superior character and understanding, in my opinion, that the labour of the day can be less properly said to be sufficient for him than he is for the labour of the day: his first ambition is that of executing it well. Intoxicated by military success, and universally pointed out as a great general (especially since the campaign of 1778, during which he all the winter maintained the feeble post of Troppau, to which the King of Prussia annexed a kind of vanity, against every effort of the Austrians), he appears effectually to have quitted military glory, to betake himself to the cares of government. Everywhere made welcome, possessed of unbounded curiosity, he still is capable of assiduously confining himself to Brunswick, and attaching himself to business. He is, in fine, a man of an uncommon stamp; but too wise to be formidable to the wise. He delights much in France, with which he is exceedingly well acquainted, and appears to be very fond of whatever comes from that country. His eldest son, returning from Lausanne, has passed through Franche-Comté, Languedoc, and Provence, and is very desirous to return to France. I shall soon know if he is to be sent back. In my opinion the son cannot be treated with too much respect there, so as to testify confidence in the father; which it seems to me would give the latter pleasure, by which he would certainly be sufficiently confirmed and flattered, to keep this treatment in memory.

I cannot at present speak of the supper, when the Duke removed me from the place of honour, opposite the Duchess, where I sat at dinner, to seat me beside himself, which is always at the far end of the table. The conversation was lively, and absolutely individual, but not political. (We had listeners.) He questioned me much concerning France. I am to dine with him to-day, and to sup with the Duchess Dowager, at Antoinetten-Ruh. I could not avoid this tax on propriety, which deprives me of an opportunity of supping with the Duke; a favour he rarely grants, and which appeared to be much remarked here, yesterday, where I am observed with anxiety. Perhaps I am supposed a place hunter.

The continuance of Zimmermann at Potsdam is prolonged, more than it was supposed it would have been. He writes that the dropsy is not confirmed, and he again talks of an asthma. This is medical cant. He is the creature of the King, not of the public. Certain it is that he has gained no victory over eel pies and *polenta*; that there are no longer any wrinkles in the face; and that the parts are all inflated and œdematous.

Prince Henry, however, is returned to Rheinsberg, where the youthful and handsome R——, as it is said, occasions rain and fair weather.

I can warrant it as a fact that a Scotchman, who is first physician to Catherine II. of Russia, being lately at Vienna, dined at the table of the Emperor, and was seated by his side. Indeed, this was avowed in the Gazettes; but it was not there avowed that, while this physician remained at Vienna, Cobenzl (the Austrian Ambassador to the Court of Petersburg, but then at Vienna) having been ordered to show the physician a pleasure house in the vicinity of the metropolis, the Emperor on horseback *happened* to meet the doctor on the road, and continued in conversation with him, at the coach window, for the space of more than two leagues.

LETTER IV

July 16th, 1786.

To-day I was three hours alone with the Duke, after rising from dinner. The conversation was animated, frank, and almost confidential: it confirmed me in most of the opinions I gave in my last letter (Number III.), but it has inspired me with much fear, concerning the situation of Prussia after the death of the King. The successor seems to have every symptom of the most incurable weakness: the most corrupt among the persons by whom he is surrounded, of whom the gloomy and visionary Bishopswerder may be ranked as first, daily increase in power. There is a coolness said to prevail between the Heir Apparent and his uncles. The coadjutorship of the order of St. John, bestowed with great solemnity on **Prince Henry**, the eldest son of **Prince Ferdinand**, which deprives the successor of more than fifty thousand crowns per annum, is the most recent cause of this coolness. It should seem that there have been very powerful intrigues for the establishment of these two young Princes, whom both city and Court regard as the children of Count Schmettau. The measures taken to effect this were strengthened at the very moment when the King was supposed to be expiring, so as to bind the successor, of whom they consequently have testified their suspicion. To the King's brother, Prince Henry, the half at least of all this appertains; nor has the Heir Apparent attempted to conceal his dissatisfaction. Thence it results that all the subaltern parties, and their dirty cabals, become more active; so that the respect in which the Court of Berlin has been held, and in which consists its greatest power, depends, perhaps, but too much on the life of the King; unless the Duke of Brunswick should seize the reins of government, the burthen of which he seriously appears to dread. In effect, a kingdom like this, which has no constituent foundation, will be cruelly agitated, should the winds of Court begin to blow; and should the Duke, who has formed himself without having studied in the school of adversity, and whose reason and sagacity it is impossible to speak too highly of, fear to reverse the whole system of his mode of life. But he does not start at difficulties ; and he is too much interested in the prosperity of Prussia not to seek to obtain influence there.

It does not appear to me probable that the first six months, or even the first year, should produce any change, or do more than prepare for change. The Duke has repeatedly assured me that all the Protestant powers of Germany, and a great part of the Catholic, would incontrovertibly be in the interest of France, whenever the latter should fully convince the Germanic body of her amicable intentions : and when I asked what pledges should be given us that the high part with which the Elector of Hanover was invested, in the confederation of the Princes, should not sway the Cabinet of Berlin to the side of the English, and should not become an invincible impediment to any sincere union between Versailles and Prussia, he clearly showed me, so as not to admit of reply, that the Germanic league would never have existed, or at least would never have assumed its present form, had it not been for the ambiguity of our conduct, relative to the Schelde, to Bavaria, and to the Oriental system. He added, that the Elector of Hanover, and the King of England, were two very distinct persons; and that the English and the Germans were great strangers to each other.

Here I ought to observe that, in my opinion, the Duke overacts his part, whenever he speaks of depressing England, which I well know he loves; and that perhaps because he feels his family connections may, in this respect, render him more liable to suspicion. In a word, I cannot too often repeat that they do not appear to have confidence in us, but that such confidence is very sincerely desired; and that the more because the Emperor, unsupported by France, is not held in the least dread, and that there is a reigning conviction he will not dare to take a single step, when the Cabinet of Versailles shall say—" We will not suffer any infraction."

Be it however remarked, that the incoherent conduct of the Emperor, and his abrupt vagaries, often unhinge all the combinations of reason. The Duke has to-day learnt a fact of this kind, which may well incite meditation.

The Baron of Gemmingen, some time since, wrote a very violent pamphlet against the German confederacy. Dohm, an excellent Prussian civilian, answered in a strong and victorious manner. The ministry of Vienna, in consequence, requested our ministry to entreat the Court of Berlin to suffer wordy hostilities to cease: the latter consented; but there has just appeared (printed indeed at Munich, but indubitably coming from Vienna) a satirical and bitter reply to Dohm. Verbal wars are rarely insignificant at Vienna; where they are never begun but under the auspices of government.

The following is another fact of serious import, if true. The Duke has received advice, from Vienna, that between four and five thousand Russians have entered Poland, where the Diet threatens to be very turbulent. The Duke is desirous we should take a decisive part, concerning and against all new arrangements tending to the further dissolution or dismemberment of Poland. I have not knowledge sufficient of this country to enter into any circumstantial detail; but I spoke to him on the subject of Courland, explaining my ideas, relative to the late proceedings of Russia in this country, such as they will be found in my memorial: and I introduced my discourse as if arising out of the conversation. He was ardently attentive to what I said, and promised to write according to my sense of the danger to Count Hertzberg. I well comprehend that the circumstances of the moment are nothing less than favourable; and the assent which was warmly given by a most excellent politician emboldens me to entreat that my memorial may be taken into consideration, though it should only be practicable in future, and that some instructions may be sent me, on the manner in which I may sound the Duke of Courland on this head, whom I shall meet at Berlin, and the principal persons of Courland, with whom I may easily correspond; my trade of traveller being known, and my desire to collect facts and to deduce consequences giving great opportunities to enquire and speak concerning all subjects.

MEMORIAL[1]

Sent to the Court of France, concerning the declaration made by Russia to Courland, and published in the "Leyden Gazettes," from the 20th of May to the 3rd of June, 1786.

COURLAND has lately been officially menaced with the indignation of the Sovereign of all the Russias; on the supposition that the report, relative to the abdication of the Duke of Courland in favour of the Prince of Wurtemberg, a general in the Prussian service, should be true.

The reigning Duke, Ernest John, a ferocious man, so much abhorred in his own country as not to be able to remain there, although he should not dread any violence from the ministry of Petersburg, is known to be the son of the famous Biron, who was reinstated Duke of Courland, in 1760, by the influence, or rather through the fear of Russia, which power, with the aid of forty

---

[1] This is apparently the memorial which is mentioned in the preceding letter.

thousand men, expelled Prince Charles of Saxony, the uncle of the Elector and the legitimate Duke, to restore the former favourite of Elizabeth,[1] whom a Court faction had lately recalled from Siberia.

It is also known that this Ernest John has more than once felt the whole weight of the resentment of Catherine II.; that he has been near twenty years banished into Siberia; that he has no influence whatever in Courland; and that his abdication is universally wished.

But it is not known, or rather it is kept secret, that he was enjoined, by a Ukase (or Edict) six years ago, to resign his duchy to Prince Potemkin; and that by the advice of the Chancellor Taubè, and of the Chamberlain Howen, he averted the storm by remitting to Prince Potemkin (whose affairs ever were and are in

---

[1] This is a mistake. Biron was the favourite of the Empress Anne Ivanowna; was banished to Siberia by Anne of Mecklenburg, the Princess Regent of Russia; was soon recalled from Schlusselburg and sent to Yaroslaf by the Empress Elizabeth; was restored to freedom by Peter III.; and, after the assassination of the latter, to his duchy by Catherine II.; not to confer a favour on Biron, but to wrest the duchy from Poland, and render it dependent on herself.

disorder) two hundred thousand ducats. Rason, the ministerial secretary of the Duke, was entrusted to carry him this sum.

Whether it be that Potemkin, while waiting for the execution of his grand projects, which perhaps relate to the Oriental system, or to circumstances that are yet immature, wishes to acquire this accession of power; whether it be that he is in want of money; or more especially whether it be that the Duke of Courland, since his situation has been so precarious, is known in consequence of his avarice to have become one of the richest Princes in Europe, and that, rendered effeminate by adversity, old age, and the daily importunities of his last wife, who has acquired some influence over him, he is endeavouring to place himself beyond the reach of ill-fortune; be it which of these causes it may, a similar crisis is again returned.

The Cabinet of Petersburg is ignorant of none of these things. It doubtless fears that the Court of Berlin is speculating, concerning the province of Courland; hoping, by the aid of a new Duke, to have it entirely at its disposal. The conditions which gave Poland a right of protection over Courland having ceased, when power became law, and at the moment the oppressed republic found it impossible to fulfil those conditions, it is not absurd to apprehend that Prussia will surreptitiously take the place of Poland, and thus to its own profit confirm the right by the deed.

Courland is in reality far from a contemptible country. Its climate, being in the 57th degree of latitude, though sufficiently is not insupportably cold. Its extent in length is eighty leagues, and in breadth fifty. Its soil is fertile, and its natural products are very necessary for all the commercial and maritime powers. Two principal and navigable rivers divide it, from east to west, the Aa and the Windau: several brooks and canals intersect it in every direction. It has two ports, Windau and Liebau on the Baltic. In its present impotent and indolent state, its commerce active and passive does not employ less than from six to seven hundred vessels, of three, four, and as far as eight hundred tons burthen. It contains seven or eight small towns, and its population is estimated at more than a million and a half of inhabitants. The land-holders may be supposed not to be in a state of wretchedness, since the revenues of the reigning Duke, whose influence in the republic is so small, annually amount to two hundred thousand pounds sterling. Such is the outline of the situation of Courland.

It would be of little use to prove, in this place, that the republic, being a free state, the Prince of which is purely elective, so that though he may abdicate he cannot transfer his privileges. Russia cannot legally interfere in the affairs of Courland, which ought to be as independent as are its rights. This word *rights* is totally stripped of meaning when opposed to the word *power*. Russia has long been in the habit of vexing Courland, internally and externally; of dictating the choice of its governors; of laying its suffrages under restraint; and of extorting or forcibly seizing on its money, its produce and its men. The Monarchs of Petersburg have always made it a principle to familiarize the Courts of Europe to the supposition that Courland has no political existence except such as Russia shall please to bestow. All this is well known.

The points I should wish briefly here to examine are:—

1. Whether it is not evidently our interest to introduce a new order of affairs; and—

2. Whether we have not the means so to do.

Courland, kept back and oppressed by every kind of exterior and interior tyranny, possesses no one species of manufacture. It abounds in naval stores; for which reason there is an affinity, resulting from circumstances, between Courland and France, which latter holds the first rank among industrious nations, or an affinity between their mutual products, the direct barter of which would give birth to the most advantageous kind of trade.

In reality, there exists at present a species of barter between Courland and France; but in so indirect a manner that it is carried on at second or third hand, by the intervention of the English, the Dutch, the Swedes, the Danes, the Prussians, the Hans-Towns, &c.

This intervention absorbs and destroys all the benefit which a trade so advantageous would be of to France, and which certainly ought abundantly to procure us, and at a moderate price, a price unknown in our dock-yards and markets, ship-timber, masts, spokes, fellies, veneering wood, &c., &c.; grain, ship-beef, salt-fish, vegetables, &c., &c. The natural returns for these would be the produce of our industry, from the coarsest to the finest articles (for nothing is manufactured in Courland) which the Courlanders (whose consumption is great, and who are very desirous of articles of luxury, and even of finery) would then obtain from us at a moderate price, still infinitely lucrative to our traders.

The advantage of this direct trade would not be confined merely to money; for, beside the influence which such intimate connections with Courland would give us in the Baltic and the North, where we should become the mediators between Prussia, Russia, and Poland, which last state must necessarily soon undergo some new change, France, by a commercial treaty with Courland, would ascertain two ports on the Baltic, which would at least remain neuter and almost exclusive to herself. These would be useful to us, both in war and peace, as depository places for stores, and most of the materials which are requisite for the royal and mercantile marine; and would highly compensate the disadvantage which continually increases, and which is preparing for us in the North, relative to our marine, in consequence of the strict connections between England and Russia.

To the attentive observer, England presents every symptom which can menace the possessions of the Dutch in the East, and which can forebode the desire of revenge. Russia can at any time rob France of a great part of the naval supplies of war, in the European seas.

This order of affairs cannot too soon be reversed.

Let it be attentively observed that there is no question here of a new treaty, but the revival of an ancient one: for the Cardinal de Richelieu made a treaty with Courland, in 1643, which was registered by the Parliament of Paris, in 1647; so that, should we at present treat with Courland, we can decisively affirm, and demonstrate, we are committing no innovation.

This seems to me to be a very important remark, which ought not a little to influence the resolution that may be taken; and the form given to that resolution, when once it is taken.

The states of Courland desire this political affinity between the two countries. The Chamberlain Howen, of whom I have spoken, is a man of the greatest influence in the republic; and, of all the Courlanders, the most anti-Russian; because that, while an envoy from Courland to the Court of Warsaw, he was carried off, by order of the Empress, and banished into Siberia. His nephew was indirectly, but formally, charged to question the government of France on this subject. I positively know he has spoken to the Count de Vergennes, and that the only answer he received from the minister was—

1. That, he being minister for foreign affairs, this was a subject that did not appertain to his department.

2. That it was requisite that the Duke of Courland and the states, conjointly and officially, should make a proposition to the King, concerning a treaty of commerce.

To this I reply—

1. That, most certainly, the minister for

foreign affairs ought to consult with the minister of finance, on whatever relates to commercial treaties; but that this does not therefore appear to me a sufficient reason to reject either the project or the proposal.

2. That it would be absurd to suppose that Courland, bowed as it is under the iron rod of present circumstances, would expose itself, by taking any open step, without first being certain its propositions should be favourably received, and that the country should be protected against that power which, possessed of strength and in the habit of taking its will for law, should make every effort to counteract, and prevent, whatever might tend to impart solidity to the constitution of Courland, and to render its political independence respectable.

I see no hope that any power, except Prussia, should interest itself in the affairs of this province. And this is the second point which it is my intention to prove, in this memorial.

1. Because the situation of the Prussian states is such that, the stability and prosperity of Courland ought no less to influence the King

of Prussia than if this country was one of his own provinces.

2. Because he cannot prudently covet Courland, which Russia would never leave him in peaceable possession of, and which would but increase the length of his provinces, already too much extended, without rendering his power more real or more compact.

This latter point is self-demonstrative; and as to the advantages which Prussia might derive from the future stability of Courland, and from the increase of its energy and industry, these are evident from a mere view of the map. Between the states of Brandenburg and Russia there is only the dismemberment of Poland, which at present forms part of Prussian Lithuania and of Courland, of which the King of Prussia, politely speaking, would become the useful proprietor that very day on which he should become its guardian and protector. Russia, therefore, necessarily and indubitably is formidable to none of the powers of Europe, Prussia excepted, on which kingdom she can bring evil, and which can do her no injury.

On the other part, it is known that there is only a very narrow slip of Polish Lithuania between the states of Prussia and Courland, which barely extends from five to six leagues. Here Prussia might easily make legal and amicable acquisitions, sufficient to open a very advantageous transport trade on the Memel, and the canals that might be cut between that river and the rivers of Courland, descending to the ports of the Baltic, of which I have spoken.

Either I am much deceived or the ministry of Berlin might easily be made to comprehend that, instead of forming projects of ambition on this republic, its real interest would be to declare, in some manner, Prussia to be the representative of Poland in her engagements towards Courland, as stipulated by the *pacta conventa* and the *pacta subjectionis*, which have been actually and necessarily destroyed. Prussia might find a hundred reasons of public right to allege, independent of her dignity and safety. This proposition, and that of acceding to our treaty of commerce with Courland, would therefore contain nothing imprudent; it would perhaps be a good means of depriving the House of Brandenburg of all fears, relative to our Northern politics. Nor does it seem to be impossible but that the King of Prussia would, on this condition, support the declaration we might make to the Court of Petersburg, that it was our determination to protect Courland; and not to suffer a free country, allied to France by ancient treaties, to be humbled, over which we would not permit any direct and legislative influence to be exerted by any court.

Such a declaration, softened by every diplomatic formality, which is so easily practised, would at this time be sufficient, in my opinion, especially if made in concert with the Court of Berlin, to repel the projects of usurpation conceived by Russia over Courland.

Be these things as they may, this small country, too little known, together with Poland and the Germanic body, claim the serious attention of the King of France; who, if my opinion be right, has no other general interest, on the continent, than that of maintaining peace and the reciprocal safety of states.

LETTER V

July 19th, 1786.

YESTERDAY morning, before my departure, the Duke granted me an audience for the space of about three hours; or rather personally indicated a conference, under the pretence of remitting letters to Berlin, and which, indeed, he committed to my care. We again spoke of general affairs, and of the particular situation of Prussia; of the suspicions which he pretends it is impossible to avoid entertaining, concerning our intentions and our system; (how should I answer him when such is the disorder of our finances that it is impossible we should have any system?) of the dread that daily increases, which the Emperor necessarily inspires, who does good awkwardly, but who does enough to acquire great power, the basis of which is magnificent, and highly disproportionate to that of any other monarchy, France excepted; of the impossibility of finding any counterpoise to this power, except in the prudence of the Cabinet of Versailles; of the little hope that the new regulations of Prussia should be wise; of the various directions which the various factions that were fermenting at Berlin might take; of the military vigour and the ambitious fumes which intoxicate the Duke of Weymar, who aspires to enter into the service of Prussia, and to embroil parties; of the necessity which there was that the Cabinet of Versailles should send a man of merit to Berlin, there to inspire awe and give advice, keep watch over the factious and the turbulent, &c., &c., &c.

At length, questioning me with an air of fearing what he was going to say was an absurdity, he asked whether I should think the project of an alliance between France, England and Prussia an impracticable chimera; the end of which, solemnly avowed, should be to guarantee, throughout Europe, to each Prince his respective possessions; a measure in itself noble, and worthy of the two first powers, which should command all others to remain at peace; founded on the evident and combined interest of the two rivals, and the greatest obstacle to which would be that no one would dare to put it in execution.

The idea, on which I have for these seven years been ruminating, is too sublime not to be seductive. It would infallibly immortalize the sovereign by whom it should be realized, and the minister by whom it should be promoted. It would change the face of Europe, and totally to our advantage: for, once again, commercial treaties, however advantageous to England, would never make the English anything more than our carriers and our most useful factors.

The Duke has permitted me to correspond with him; he even desired me so to do, and I find I have obtained almost that very place in his opinion which I myself could have wished.

July 21*st*, 1786.

First Postscript.—I am arrived, and perhaps I shall learn but little to-day. The dropsy is in the stomach; nay, in the lungs. He was informed of it on Thursday. He heard it with great magnanimity, say some; others affirm he treated the physician, who was too sincere, very ill. He might drag on life, if he would take advice, Doctor Baylies says, another year; but I suspect he will never give up eel-pies. Count Hertzberg has been at Sans-Souci this week past; he had never before been sent for. Two days previous to that on which the King made him this kind of honourable reparation, if, however, it be anything else than the necessity of giving breath to those who are obliged to converse with him, and of enlivening his conversation, the Heir Apparent dined with the Count at his country seat, and passed best part of the evening with him and the Prince of Dessau. This has bewildered the parties that are hotly animated against this estimable minister, in and for whom, according to my opinion, our embassy has always testified too little confidence and respect.

Second Postscript.—I have intelligence, from what I believe to be a very certain and profound source, wholly independent of the Cabinet of Berlin, that the Emperor has made preparations which greatly menace those parts of Moldavia and Wallachia that would be convenient to him to possess; that he is immediately expected to repair to those frontiers in person; and that such motions cannot otherwise be explained than by re-acting the conquest of the Crimea in those countries. This information, combined with the ultimatum which Russia has delivered in to the Porte, seems to me to be of sovereign importance. I do not know the precise intentions of the Court of France; but, if the indefinite aggrandizement of the Emperor and particularly the execution of the Oriental system are as formidable to us as I suppose them to be, I entreat deliberations may be held whether it befits the dignity of the King to suffer the tragedy of Poland to recommence, the interest of the state to lose the Levant trade, or prudent policy to temporize, when the match is putting to the touch-hole. I cannot for my own part doubt but that our inactivity, in such a case, must be gratuitous; because that the Emperor would most certainly not brave us; and fatal also, since we are precisely the only power who have at once the interest and the strength to impede such attempts. England will trouble herself little concerning them, and without us Prussia is nothing.

LETTER VI

July 21st, 1786.

An odd incident has happened to me. I am just returned from the French ambassador's, who sent me word he could not have the honour of receiving my visit, because he was busy. To feel the whole import of this act, it is necessary to know that there has lately appeared an article in the *Hamburg Gazette,* affirming in express terms I had received orders to quit France. You will further recollect that, in general, the ambassador of France is eagerly desirous of receiving the visits of French travellers. Such is the present combination of circumstances that this, which would only, on any other occasion, be an affair of rather serious impoliteness, is at this moment a very embarrassing affectation. I believe I have no need to tell you I am far superior to punctilio; but this is not mere form. The natural preponderance of France is such that the respect in which a native of that country is held cannot be wholly independent of the reception he shall meet from the ambassador. What then must be thought when he shall be envied, suspected and watched; and when pretences are sought to render his character equivocal? And what must be his situation, when, far from seeking to quarrel with the ambassador, it is his duty and his wish, on all occasions, to preserve appearances, and to protect him from becoming instead of making him ridiculous?

You will have no difficulty in comprehending that it is an intricate affair, and that I must well reflect on the part I have to take. At present I must dissemble, and expose myself to a new refusal to-morrow; but it will be impossible to suffer this new refusal to remain unnoticed. I write you word of this in order that, in any case, and rather too soon than too late, you should inform M. d'Esterno it is not the intention of government that I should be treated in a disrespectful manner, and still less as a proscribed person. He is so much of a timid trembler, that he may have been imposed upon by the Hamburg paragraph. I do not think him sufficiently cunning to have written it himself.

He certainly appeared ridiculously disturbed at my return, and entirely departed from his silent circumspection, that he might discover, by questioning those whom he supposed intimate with me, what were my intentions. Some of the numerous persons who do not love him, especially among the *corps diplomatique*, have amused themselves with inventing tales relative to my views, similar to those of the "Thousand and One Nights." His brain is in a state of fermentation upon the subject; and the more so as he is acting out of character. I may in consequence of this be very ill-situated here: to prevent this you will take proper measures.—I shall tell you more before I seal this letter: he is not a person who will oppose the least ministerial insinuation.

LETTER VII

July 23rd, 1786.

THERE is nobody here, consequently I shall for some days lead an inactive life. There is no Court, except that of Prince Ferdinand, which is always insignificant: he is at present on the recovery.[1] Prince Frederick of Brunswick knows nothing. The English Embassy caress and suspect me. Count Hertzberg still remains at Sans-Souci; I must therefore satisfy myself with the sterility of the moment. I imagine I have discovered that the real occasion of the threatening declaration of Russia, respecting Courland, was a secret proposal of marriage between the Countess of Würtemberg, the natural daughter of the Duke, and a Prussian; and the increasing intimacy of the Duke with the Heir Apparent, who has found in the purse of this savage Scythian that pecuniary aid with which he ought long since to have been supplied by France. The

---

[1] Prince Ferdinand had just then escaped from a dangerous fit of sickness.

Duke of Courland departed, soon after the menace of Petersburg appeared, with his wife, who is said to be pregnant, to drink the Pyrmont waters. According to all appearances, instead of remaining at Berlin on his return, he will go to Mittau. He still continues to make acquisitions in the Prussian dominions: he has lately bought the county of Sagan, in Silesia; and the King, who was not a little vexed to see the Prince of Lobkowitz spend the revenues of this fine estate at Vienna, treats the Duke of Courland with great favour. Beside remitting the manor fees, he consented to alienate or at least to entail the fief on female descendants, which before was reversible to the crown on the want of male heirs; so that the Duke, who has no son, found that, by his carelessness, or a very strange kind of ignorance, he had risked six hundred thousand German crowns on a chance the most hazardous.

It is indubitable that Prince Potemkin is, or appears to be, more in favour than ever. It has been found necessary to approve his disobedience. There are reports that he has sought a reconciliation with the Grand Duke, which he has accomplished.

The new minister of Petersburg (the son of Field-Marshal Romanzow) is not successful here: intelligent people, however, affirm he possesses understanding and information. I know he has strong prejudices against me, which I shall endeavour to remove, and to gain his intimacy; for he is of such a nature that much may be derived from his acquaintance. But you must feel I stand in need of some instructions, or at least of a series of questions, which shall serve me as a compass, and by which I may obtain the customary intelligence. General politics have for some years been very incoherent, for want of possessing some fixed system.—Which of the two alliances, that of the House of Austria, or that between the two Imperial Courts, Austria and Russia, ought to be regarded as stable, sacred, and subordinate to the other? Is France resolved to quit her natural train, I mean to say her continental system, for the maritime? If so, whether wisely or not, this will at least explain our extreme cautiousness, in what relates to the projects of the Court of Vienna.

The man who wants this knowledge can do little more than wander at a venture; he may, with more or less intelligence, write a gazette, but, not having a sufficient basis to build on, cannot be a negotiator. I entreat it may not be supposed I have the presumption to interrogate: I only mean to explain, in very few words, such of the reasons which, exclusive of my own want of capacity, and of the few means my situation affords me, infinitely circumscribe that utility which I wish and labour to be of to my country.

I hope I shall not be suspected of supposing any importance annexed to those extracts from the German newspapers, which I shall in future send by every courier. It is purely an object of curiosity, but which I thought might be agreeable in a country where, I believe, not a single German gazette is received; and into which so many ambassadors send no other despatches than those obtained on the authority of these gazettes. I shall only speak in my extracts of the news of the North.

First Postscript.—Advice yesterday arrived commanding Lord Dalrymple to depart, and bear the order of the garter to the Landgrave of Hesse Cassel.

Second Postscript.—I have received a very friendly letter from Sans-Souci. The King seems to hope he shall still live long, he appears, however, to be much more occupied concerning himself and his pine-apples than by foreign affairs. Astonishment is testified (this is a surprising affair!) though in a very obliging manner, that the son of the Count de Vergennes should pass through Hamburg, Dresden, Vienna, &c., without any hope of seeing him at Berlin. I have answered I was very grateful, in behalf of my nation, for the importance annexed to the topographical peregrination of the son of our minister for foreign affairs; and that I imagined nothing could be more flattering to his father; but that, for my own part, I was wholly uninformed on the subject; though I was persuaded that, if the Court of Berlin was reserved as the last place to be visited, it would only be from a love of the *Crescendo*. I said the same to Count Goertz, by whom I was warmly questioned.

LETTER VIII

Berlin, July 26th, 1786.

THE fine weather supports the life of the King, but he is ill. On Wednesday he was for some minutes wheeled about in his chair, by which he was much incommoded, and suffered greatly during and after the exercise. His pains increased on Thursday, and yesterday he was no better. I persist in my opinion that the period of his existence will be towards the month of September.

The Heir Apparent does not quit Potsdam, where he keeps on the watch. Still the same respectful passion for Mademoiselle Voss.[1] During a short journey that she lately made with her brother, a confidential valet-de-chambre followed her carriage at a distance, and if the beauty, who in my opinion is very ordinary, testified the least desire (to eat white bread, for example) before she had proceeded half a league further,

---

[1] At present the Countess of Ingenheim.

she found everything she wished. It appears indubitable that she has not yet yielded. No great use can be made either of her uncle or her brothers. Frenchwomen arrive daily; but I doubt much whether there will be any great advantage derived from them, except to innkeepers and milliners.

The Duke of Courland has lent the Heir Apparent money to pay his debts at Berlin; they are supposed to be all discharged, except those of his Princess, which they are not very anxious to liquidate, from the fear of giving her bad habits.

I have spoken at large with Struensee. He supposes the project of the bank to be a grand and superb operation, which cannot but succeed. He asks timely information, and promises to place and cause to be placed in it a considerable sum; but the secret must only be known to him, and the subject treated only between ourselves.

LETTER IX

July 31*st*, 1786.

I SUPPOSE in reality that, in this commencement of correspondence, my letters are waited for, in order to write to me; however, if my letter of the 23rd of July (Number V.) has been well deciphered and considered, it cannot be disowned that I stand in need of instructions. Politics are at a crisis. I repeat, politics are at a crisis. It is impossible they should continue as they are; whether it be from endeavours to accelerate or efforts to retard. Everything denotes the Oriental system to increase in vigour. I have no doubt but that, soon or late, it will be destructive of that of the West; and the danger is immediate, is instantaneous. If Turkey in Europe, speaking in political and commercial language, be one of our colonies, if we are not resolved to leave it to its fate, is it not time to pay it some attention, and because that it is so, the general system of Europe out of the question? Were the King of Prussia ten years younger, he would well know how to restore the equilibrium; for he would take as much from Poland as others might take elsewhere: but he dies and has no successor. For my own part, it is easy to conceive I shall consume my time in barren efforts; and, after taking much more trouble, shall be much less useful than if I knew what track to follow, and where to gain information.

The King is in daily danger of death, though he may live some months. I persist in my autumnal prognostics. Prince Henry having sent for me to Rheinsberg by a very formal and friendly letter, it would appear affectation in me not to go; and I shall set off on Wednesday, after the departure of the courier. I shall not remain there longer than a week, where I shall have good opportunities of intelligence concerning the state of the King, and of gaining information on various matters.

Postscript.—The King is sensibly worse: he has had a fever these two days; this may kill him, or prolong his life. Nature has continually done so much for this extraordinary man, that nothing more is wanting to restore him than a hemorrhoidal eruption. The muscular powers are very great.

The English Embassy has received advice from Vienna that the Emperor is in Transylvania, and that the world is ignorant of what he is doing, what he intends, or even to what place he is gone.

All the boats on the Danube are taken into his service.

* *

The maritime company wished to monopolize the sale of snuff and tobacco in Sweden, offering to pay half-a-million annually to the King; but the Swedish states have totally refused to forbid the cultivation of tobacco in the kingdom, and this was the condition, *sine quâ non*. The actions of this Monarch decline greatly, on all occasions; another Diet like the present, and monarchical power would once more fall in Sweden. It appears to be undoubted that the rumour of his having turned Catholic, on his journey to Rome, has alienated the whole nation. But are we to impute nothing to the intrigues of Russia, in the present fermentation?

Struensee repeats that, if the bank be established, he and his friends are ready; that is to say, the most monied men in the kingdom: and probably, under a new reign, the government itself. This man ought to be cherished: it would be of importance were I often empowered to give him good information respecting the state of the place. Meditate on this. His resources are in himself, and will probably survive his administration. He has gained immensely, by speculating in the English funds: he ought to be weaned of this, to which he is self-inclined, for he feels and owns that chances in the English funds are exhausted, for the remainder of his life.

LETTER X

August 2nd, 1786.

Written before my departure for Rheinsberg.

THE King is evidently better, at least with respect to pain, when he does not move; he has even left off the use of the *taraxicum,* or dandelion, the only thing Zimmermann prescribed, who, consequently, is in despair. He simply takes a tincture of rhubarb mixed with diarrhœtics, which give him copious evacuations. His appetite is very good, which he indulges without restraint. The most unhealthy dishes are his greatest favourites. If indigestion be the consequence, as it frequently is, he takes a double aperitive dose.

Frese, his physician of Potsdam, still continues in disgrace, for having dared to whisper the word dropsy on the question being asked him, and an appeal made to his conscience, what was the name and character of the disease. The King is exceedingly chilly, and is continually enveloped in furs, and covered by feather-beds. He has not entered his bed these six weeks, but is removed from one arm-chair to another, in which he takes tolerably long sleeps, turned on his right side. Inflation augments; the scrotum is exceedingly tumid. He perceives this, but will not persuade himself, or appear to believe, that it is anything more than the inflation of convalescence, and the result of great feebleness.

This information is minutely exact, and very recent. There is no doubt of his unwillingness to die. The people best informed think that, as soon as he believes himself really dropsical and at the point of death, he will submit to be tapped, and to the most violent remedies, rather than peaceably resign himself to sleep with his fathers. He even desired, some time since, incisions might be made in his hams and thighs; but the physician feared to risk them. With respect to his understanding, it is still sound; and he even continues his labours.

LETTER XI

August 8th, 1786.

THE King is dangerously ill; some affirm he has not many hours to live, but this probably partakes of exaggeration. On the fourth, the erysipelas with blisters on the legs made their appearance: this prognosticates bursting, and soon after gangrene. At present there is suffocation, and a most infectious smell. The smallest fever— and the curtain must drop.

LETTER XII

August 12th, 1786.

THE King is apparently much better. The evacuation, which was the consequence of the apertures in his legs, has caused the swelling to abate, and given ease; but has been followed by a dangerous excess of appetite. He cannot continue in this state. You may expect to receive a grand packet at my return from Rheinsberg.

LETTER XIII

August 15th, 1786.

I AM just returned from Rheinsberg, where I have lived in the utmost familiarity with Prince Henry. I have numerous modes of communication, which will develop themselves as time and opportunity shall serve; at present I shall only state consequences.

Prince Henry is in the utmost incertitude, concerning what he shall or shall not be under the new reign. He greatly dreads, and more than he wishes to appear to dread, though his fears are very visible, the influence of Count Hertzberg, who is still detained at Sans-Souci, but, as I think, only for the sake of his conversation—at least, as far as respects the old King. This Count Hertzberg has openly espoused the English system; but though the flatteries of Ewart[1] and his secret arts have much profited

---

[1] Then Secretary to the Embassy, and now the English Ambassador at Berlin.

by the long contempt in which the French Embassy have held this minister, I believe his principal reason for attaching himself to England is because that Prince Henry, his implacable enemy, is the avowed and fanatical protector of the French system; and because the Count imagines he cannot otherwise make himself indispensably necessary to the opposite party; for which reason he clothes himself in the uniform of the Stadtholder.

In consequence of this, and persuaded as I am that Prince Henry has not sufficient influence over the successor (who is weary of avuncular despotism) to displace Hertzberg, who will continually batter his enemy in breach, by boasting, by meannesses, by a faithful portrait of the Prince's creatures, and by the jealousy with which he will inspire the new King against Prince Henry, who, if he be anything, will be master; convinced also that he (Hertzberg) is useful to France, which is influenced by the uncle because he holds the English system in abhorrence, I have exerted every effort to induce Prince Henry (who wants nothing but dissimulation) to reconcile himself with Count Hertzberg, and thus put his nephew out of fear. This he might with the greater security do, because that Hertzberg, relative to him, could be nothing more than a first clerk, who, if he should act uprightly, would make as good a clerk as another; and who, should he endeavour to deceive, might be the more easily crushed, after having been admitted a colleague.

I have had much difficulty in persuading him, for Baron Knyphausen, the brother-in-law of Hertzberg, and his irreconcilable enemy, because that their interests clash, is possessed of the entire political confidence of the Prince; of which he is worthy, for he is a very able man, and perhaps the only able man in Prussia; but as he is in danger of a confirmed palsy as his mind and body both decay, and as the Prince himself perceives they do, I was able to effect my purpose by dwelling on all these circumstances, while I heaped exaggerated praise on Baron Knyphausen, and expressed infinite regret for his situation; so that I have prevailed on the Prince, and have personally received a commission to negotiate an accommodation, between him and Hertzberg; for which purpose I shall go the day after to-morrow to Potsdam.

What may I augur from all this? Weakness only and incoherency. It appears indubitable that petty cabals, the fine arts, the blues, the subalterns, the wardrobe, and particularly the mystics, will engross the new King. I have anecdotes innumerable on this subject, by which I shall endeavour to profit, and which I shall communicate in good time. Has he any system? I believe not. Any understanding? Of that I doubt. Any character? I cannot tell: my present opinion is that no conclusions, for or against, ought yet to be drawn.

To memorials exceedingly well-drawn up by Prince Henry and Baron Knyphausen, all tending to demonstrate that, should Prussia attach itself to the English system, fifteen years hence Frederick William will be the Marquis of Brandenburg, he gives replies which are slow, vague, laconic, and hieroglyphic. He wrote the other day, for example (I saw the letter), "*The Prince of the Asturias is all English.*" Baron Boden, however, who is his confidential correspondent, and who has lately remained shut up with him a whole week in his garden at

Potsdam, has protested that the dispositions of the successor are wholly French, and that he had charged him to endeavour to convert Hertzberg. Remark this. Remark, still further, that Boden is a man of low cunning, who may wish to deceive Prince Henry, in whose service he formerly was, with whom he quarrelled, and to whom he is now reconciled; Heaven knows by what means. Observe, once again, that the Prince of Salm-Kirburg has also been (nearly about the same time) a week concealed at Potsdam. What inconsistency!

It is the advice of Prince Henry that Boden, who is returned to Paris, should be tampered with. He also wishes (for your great men do not disdain little means) that a lady should be sent hither, of a fair complexion, rather fat, and with some musical talents, who should pretend to come from Italy, or anywhere but France; who shall have had no public amour; who should appear rather disposed to grant favours than to display her poverty, &c., &c. Some elegant trifles would not be amiss; but take care not to forget the man is avaricious. The French letters, at least those which I shall shew, ought to speak well of him ; and to report that the King has spoken favourably of him ; particularly that he has said — " This Prince, like me, will be a worthy man." Repetition might be made of the success of Prince Henry in France ; but in this I would advise moderation, for I believe Prince Henry has spoken too much himself on that subject ; he has pretended to prophesy concerning the new reign, and predictions are disagreeable. Let me add it is affirmed that, could the new King be gained, he would become the most faithful and the most fervent of allies : to this his uncle Henry pledges his honour and his head ; and, indeed, the Prince of Prussia has never forfeited his word. It is added, as you may well believe, that it is neither possible nor proper to require more, for in fine we are suspected, and with good reason, &c., &c.

You will imagine France has not been thus treated without any pleadings in the behalf of Prussia ; and the advocates have pretended to prove (the map on the table) alike by military and political details, that the alliance of Prussia would be much more effectual to France, against

England, than that of Austria. If it be requested, I will draw up a memorial, according to the grounds that have been given me. Nor is it at all required that we should quarrel with Vienna: nothing more is asked than a treaty of confraternity, agreeable to the guarantee of the treaty of Westphalia; a treaty well known at all Courts, and with this only secret article that, should there be any infringement of the peace, we then should go further; and if at the present a treaty should be refused, reciprocal letters between the two Kings, sealed and so left till some event should happen, would be deemed satisfactory. In short, a pledge is demanded against the Austrian system; and the written word of honour of the King of France will be accepted. No subsidies are or will in any case be asked; perhaps even Prussia will pay subsidies to Brunswick and Hesse. Great complaints are made of France for having permitted and even favoured the German confederation. "For must not Germany, soon or late, assume some consistent form? Must not Prussia acquire a frontier? And what other means are there than those of secularization, which by this confederacy are interdicted? How otherwise arrange the affairs of Saxony than by Westphalia and Liège?" This latter phrase appeared to me very remarkable.

※ ※ ※

I do not nor cannot at present mean to send anything more than the great outlines. Prince Henry is French, and so will live and die. Will he have any influence? I know not. He is too pompous; and the Duke of Brunswick, of a very different complexion, is the man necessary to the King and the country, though he is not loved by the former. However, I am supplied with the secret means of correspondence, enquiry, and success; and it could not be more made a common cause between us. I am promised that my services to my country shall be amply repaid on the day an alliance is concluded with France, &c., &c.

I forgot a curious fact. The Heir Apparent wrote to Boden, before his journey to Berlin, to enquire what the people of Paris thought of him. "That you will be feeble, indolent, and governed," was the substance of Boden's reply.

The Prince, as he read the letter, stamped with his foot, and exclaimed, "F———[1], I have suffered by myself and I will reign by myself."

Postscript.—By the natural discharge of the water from the legs, which may be calculated at a pint per diem, the swelling of the scrotum has disappeared : the patient imagines the general inflation is diminished. It is probable he is feverish every night ; but of this he endeavours to remain ignorant. His appetite is so extraordinary that he generally eats of ten or twelve of the highest dishes. His supper and breakfast consist of smoked tongues, bread, butter, and a large quantity of pepper. If he feel his stomach oppressed by its load, which is usually the case; he has recourse an hour or two after dinner to a dose of *anima rhei*. He wishes to have six or seven motions in the twenty-four hours, exclusive of clysters. From all this you may gather the result, which is that we are incontestibly at the last scene, more or less protracted.

---

[1] An obscene, dirty French exclamation.

LETTER XIV

August 17*th*, 1786.

ALL is over!—Frederick William reigns—and one of the grandest characters that ever occupied the throne has burst one of the finest moulds that nature ever organized!

The vanity of friendship was highly interested that you should be the first informed of this event; and my measures were all most carefully taken. On Wednesday, at eight in the morning, I knew he was as ill as possible; that the preceding day the hour of appointment for the day following was noon, instead of eleven o'clock, as was before customary; that he had not spoken to his secretaries till mid-day, who had been waiting from five in the morning; that, however, the dispatches had been clear and precise; and that he still had eaten excessively, and particularly a lobster. I further knew that the prodigious foulness of the sick chamber, and the damp clothes of the patient, which he wore without changing, appeared to have brought on a species of putrid fever; that the slumbers of this Wednesday approached lethargy; that every symptom foreboded an apoplectic dropsy, a dissolution of the brain; and that, in fine, the scene must close in a few hours.

At one o'clock I took an airing on horseback, on the road to Potsdam, impelled by I know not what foreboding, and also to observe the meanderings of the river, which is on the right, when a groom, riding full speed, came for the physician Zelle, who received orders to make all haste, and who instantly departed. I soon was informed that the groom had killed a horse.

I was thrown into some perplexity. That the city gates would be shut was certain; it was even possible that the draw-bridges of the island of Potsdam would be raised the moment death should take place, and should this happen my uncertainty would continue as long as it should please the new King. On the first supposition— how send off a courier? There were no means of scaling the ramparts or the palisadoes, without being exposed to a fray, for there are sentinels at every forty paces behind the palisadoes, and at every fifty behind the wall. What was to be done? I had not received, could not receive any orders; I could only use my own resources. And ought I to expose myself to ridicule, by sending intelligence already known, or concerning an event so well foreseen? Was the loss or gain of a week worth the expense of a courier? Had I been ambassador, the certain symptoms of mortality would have determined me to have sent off an express before death. For what addition was the word death? How was I to act in my present situation? It certainly was most important to serve, and not merely to appear to have served. —I hastened to the French Ambassador. He was not at home: he dined at Charlottenburg. No means of joining him at Berlin. I dressed myself, hurried to Schoenhausen, and arrived at the palace of the Queen as soon as the ambassador. He had not been informed of particulars, and did not imagine the King was so ill; not a minister believed it; the Queen had no suspicion of it; she only spoke to me of my dress, of Rheinsberg, and of the happiness she had there enjoyed when Princess Royal. Lord Dalrymple, with whom I am too intimate to admit of dissembling what my opinion was, assured me I was deceived. "That may be," replied I: but I whispered to our ambassador that I had my intelligence from the sick couch, and that he ought to believe stock-jobbers had as good information as the diplomatic body.[1] I know not whether he believed me; but, like me, he would not sit down to play, and left the company soon enough to send news of the approach of death.

I still had great reason to be diffident of the activity of our embassy. How did I act? I sent a man, on whom I could depend, with a strong and swift horse to a farm, four miles from Berlin, from the master of which I had some days before received two pair of pigeons, an experiment on the flight of which had been made; so that, unless the bridges of the isle of Potsdam were raised, I acted with certainty: and, that I might not have a single chance against me, for I thought the news

---

[1] It will here be perceived this was intended to give the French Ambassador to understand that he had no competitor.

tardy in arriving, I sent M. de Noldé by the daily stage, with orders to wait at the bridges of the island. He was acquainted with the station of my other man; the raising of the bridges would speak plainly enough; he had money sufficient to push forward; there was no human power apparently that could counteract me, for my gentry had not a single Prussian post to pass, and were to proceed to Saxony, taking care not to go through any fortified place; and they had their route ready traced.

M. de Noldé was departing at half-past six in the morning, with the stage, when General Goertz, aide-de-camp to the late King, arriving full speed, called aloud — " In the King's name, lower the portcullis," and M. de Noldé was obliged to turn back! Five minutes after, I was on horseback; my horses had passed the night saddled; and, that I might omit nothing, I hastened to the French Ambassador. He was asleep. I wrote to him immediately that I knew a certain mode of conveyance, if he had anything to send. He answered, and I keep his note as a curious proof if, which however to me appears impossible, the

Count de Vergennes keeps no courier[1]—" The Count d'Esterno has the honour to return thanks to Mirabeau, but cannot profit by his obliging offer."

I then reflected, either he had sent off a courier, who only could convey the news of the King's extreme danger, consequently there must be something to add, or he had received orders not to send any; otherwise his apathy was wholly inconceivable. I, moreover, knew that the Saxon envoy had sent off his chasseur on the eve, so that he was twenty hours and forty leagues in advance with me; it therefore was wholly improbable that M. de Vibraye at Dresden should not hear of the King's danger. The same might be conjectured of the aide-de-camp Wittinkoff, who bore the news to the Duchess Dowager of Brunswick, and would certainly spread it, so that nothing was left for me till absolute death should happen. After considering, I did not find we were rich enough to throw a hundred guineas away; I therefore renounced all my fine projects, which

---

[1] The Count de Vergennes first read the news in the *Leyden Gazette*.

had cost me some thought, some trouble, and some guineas; and I let fly my pigeons to my man with the word RETURN.

Have I done well, or ill? Of this I am ignorant; but I had no express orders, and sometimes works of supererogation gain but little applause. I have thought it my duty to send you this account; first, because it may be of service (observe that several prizes have thus been gained); and secondly, to prove that I wanted neither zeal nor activity, but effrontery.

The new King remained all Thursday at Sans-Souci, in the apartment of General Moellendorf. His first act of sovereignty was to bestow the order of the Black Eagle on Count Hertzberg. At five in the morning, His Majesty was busy with the secretaries of the late King. This morning he was on horseback in the streets of Berlin, accompanied by his eldest son. Thursday presented a spectacle worthy of observation.

There were many wet eyes, even among foreign ambassadors; for they were all present, the French excepted, when the troops took the oath of allegiance.

The ceremony is awful, and would be more so if the oath, which the soldiers repeat word by word, were not so long. Yet this vast military paraphernalia, that multitude of soldiers, who all the morning swarmed in the streets, and the precipitate administering of the legionary oath, seem but to me too exclusively to proclaim the military power: seem but to say—I AM MORE ESPECIALLY THE KING OF THE SOLDIERS. I COMMIT MYSELF TO MY ARMY, BECAUSE I AM NOT CERTAIN OF POSSESSING A KINGDOM.—I am persuaded these military forms will be mitigated under the new reign.

LETTER XV

August 18*th*, 1786.

Prince Henry received information of the decease somewhat late; not till yesterday, the seventeenth, at midnight. But this, perhaps, was occasioned by their desire to send him one of his favourite officers, who was a very bad horseman. The letter of the King was a page and a half in length, written by his own hand, and inviting the Prince to come, who arrived to-day at three in the afternoon. As soon as it was dark, his aide-de-camp came for me; and what follows is the substance of the Prince's narrative.

He has had an interview of an hour and a half with the King, but is no further advanced in the knowledge of what he shall hereafter be. The King was devoid of ostentation in his behaviour to his family; and was very much moved with the Prince, says the latter, but no way communicative. The uncle only attempted to speak of foreign politics. His request in behalf of his favourite, Tauensien, captain and aide-de-camp to his Royal Highness, was immediately granted.

"Resolved on the French system, but desirous of seeing "—" Why ? "—" Dignity, prudence, the alarming discontents of Holland."—"Are you brother or King ?—As brother interest yourself—As King do not interfere, you will but have the greater influence."—" Your father, whose name you cannot pronounce without weeping, was as much French as I am ; this I will demonstrate by his letters."—" Oh, I have seen proofs of that," replied the King, " in those of the Queen of Sweden."

" Vienna."—" Advances it is supposed will be made ; they will be accepted ; the war of peace will actually be concluded."

" The English system ? "—" God preserve me from it."[1]—" Russia ? "—" It has scarcely been thought on."

The whole day passed in well-managed artifice. The King was on horseback with his eldest son ; he addressed his generals with caresses of every kind—" If you serve less faith-

---

[1] It is Hertzberg who debates warmly for Holland ; and beneath this mask the tip of the English ear appears.

fully than formerly, I, by being obliged to punish, shall be the person punished." He spoke a little more seriously to the ministers, with whom, notwithstanding, he dined.—Severely to the secretaries —" I well know you have been guilty of indiscretions: I would advise you to change your behaviour."

Hertzberg hitherto preserves all his consequence. The King has not once pronounced his name to Prince Henry, nor the Prince to the King. His Majesty, however, tenderly embraced Count Finckenstein, a true French knight errant, and the only person, after Knyphausen, in whom Prince Henry confides; that is to say, willingly.— " I thank you," said the King, " for the eminent services you have been so indefatigable in rendering my uncle; and I request you will act in the same manner for my interest——." It is to be noted that Count Finckenstein is the implacable enemy of Hertzberg, but the uncle of the dearly beloved Mademoiselle Voss.

The will is to be opened to-morrow, in presence of those interested. The King will not attempt to alter a single line, one article excepted, the necessity of erasing which he will submit to his uncles. The old Monarch has been generous. He has bequeathed Prince Henry two hundred thousand crowns and a handsome ring, exclusive of what will revert to him by the family agreement. The rest are likewise well treated, but not so magnificently.

The funeral ceremony afforded Prince Henry a proper excuse for remaining; it is to be performed at Potsdam. The King will depart thence to receive homage in Prussia and Silesia; this is an old custom of the country. Prince Henry will come to an explanation previous to his journey; but he is determined to wait as long as possible, that the King may begin the subject himself.

Speaking of me, his Majesty said—"I suspect he is ordered to observe me; his love[1] for the Emperor probably will not expose him to the temptation of speaking ill of me, when there is nothing ill to be spoken."

Prince Henry fears that, the mode of life excepted, the method and especially the ceremonies of government will be continued. He

---
[1] This is ironical.

has charged me to mention that Count d'Esterno is much too cold, too distant, too entirely an ambassador, for the new King. He entreats our ministry not to be tedious in bargaining concerning the pledges of confidence.

It is said, and I forgot to ask Prince Henry, who perhaps does not know whether it be or be not true, that the King has sent for the Duke of Brunswick. The minister, Schulemburg, is in danger. Prince Henry, by whom he has so long been hated and decried, is resolved to give him support. Schulemburg only returned this morning. He has composed, or rather made Struensee compose, an apologetic memorial, adroit and sophistical, in which he has imputed to the late King that order of affairs which he proposes to remedy. He declaims against monopolies: he, who is himself at the head of all the monopolies; but he endeavours to prove they cannot be suddenly reformed, especially that of the maritime company.

LETTER XVI

August 22nd, 1786.

PRINCE HENRY is singularly well satisfied with the new King, who the day before yesterday (Sunday) spent the greatest part of the afternoon with his uncle. The latter went to him in the morning to know the watchword. He pretends his nephew indicates an entire confidence in him; but I fear he interprets compliments into pledges of trust. He affirms the downfall of Hertzberg approaches; this I do not believe. "I and my nephew," said the Prince, "have been very explicit"; but I doubt the nephew has deceived the uncle. The conciliating temper of the King, and his good-nature, which induce him to receive all with kindness, may likewise lead to error, without intending deception; and these rather prove he possesses sensibility than strength of mind.

Prince Henry affirms the King is entirely French. He requests that no attention may be paid to the sending of Colonel or Major Geysau to London, with accession compliments; these, he affirms, relate only to the family. The King has beside been deceived: he was told that the Court of St. James had sent compliments at the death of King George, which is not true. This, it is added, is an artifice of Count Hertzberg. Prince Henry did not arrive soon enough to prevent the thing being done; were it to do again it should be otherwise. (Remark, it is the Prince himself who speaks.) No one has been sent either to Vienna or to Petersburg. (Not to Vienna, to the chief of the empire, who is almost as near a relation as the King of England. And as to Petersburg, Romanzow has made such bitter complaints that Count Finckenstein, moderate as he is, demanded whether he had received orders from his Court to speak in that style.) But it is singular enough that envoys have been sent everywhere else; and particularly Count Charles Podewils (brother of him who is at Vienna) is gone to bear the news to Sweden. This is departing from the old system, to which, it is said, the King means, in other respects, to adhere; for the King of Sweden was held in aversion by the late King; nor is he less hated by Prince Henry. Count

Stein, a kind of domestic favourite, is gone to Saxony, Weymar, Deux-Ponts, &c.

Prince Henry wishes the minister for foreign affairs should write, and immediately, that the Court of France hopes the new King will confirm the friendship his predecessor began; and should give it to be understood that all the Prussian ministers are not supposed to mean as well, toward France, as the King himself—(I am not at all of this opinion; for this would be to distinguish Hertzberg, and to render the war against our Cabinet more inveterate. If the downfall of this minister be necessary, it can only be effected by taxing him with governing the King)—and that the reciprocity of goodwill and good offices may, and ought to, produce a more intimate connection. He wishes M. de Calonne might write soon to him (Prince Henry) a friendly and ostensible letter, but which ought to be sent by safe hands; that it should be recommended to Count d'Esterno to smooth his brow; and he is particularly desirous a mode of somewhat calming the affairs of Holland should be found, and that this act should be much praised and insisted on.

The Duke of Brunswick has been sent for, and is to arrive on Thursday. It is said he brings another will, which was deposited in his hands. The first was not read before the family, but only in presence of the two uncles and the two ministers. The legatees have all received their bequests. The date of this will is 1769. It is in a pompous style, and is written with labour and declamation. The King has been exceeding attentive to specify that his legacies are made from the savings of his privy purse.

The following is a sketch of his donations. The Queen has an annual augmentation to her income of ten thousand crowns. Prince Henry has the gross sum of two hundred thousand crowns, a large green diamond, a lustre of rock crystal estimated at fifteen thousand crowns, a set of eight coach-horses, two led horses richly caparisoned, and fifty *anteaux*, or small casks of Hungarian wine. Prince Ferdinand the gross sum of fifty thousand crowns, and some Hungarian wine. Princess Ferdinand ten thousand crowns annually (the reason of this was that, in 1769, she was the only Princess of her house who had any children) and a box. Princess Henry six thousand crowns annually. The Duchess Dowager of Brunswick ten thousand crowns annually. The Princess Amelia ten thousand crowns annually, and all the personal plate of the late King. The Princess of Würtemberg the gross sum of twenty thousand crowns. The Duke of Würtemberg a ring. The Landgrave of Hesse the gross sum of ten thousand crowns. Prince Frederick of Brunswick the same. The reigning Duke of Brunswick the same, with eight horses (among others, the last that Frederick mounted) and a diamond ring, estimated at twenty-two thousand crowns, &c., &c., &c.

The King has confirmed all this with a very good grace. The only article that he will not agree to was a strange whim of the late King, relative to the interment of his body; he wished to be buried beside his dogs. Such is the last mark of contempt which he thought proper to cast upon mankind.[1] I know not whether the will

---

[1] The tongue of scandal *very publicly*, that is to say, in Prussia, gives a far different reason; but it is one so revolting, so atrocious, that not only charity but probability

that is coming will be equally respected with that already opened, even though they should not be contradictory.

As to the situation of the Court, I believe the truth to be that Prince Henry exaggerates his ascendancy; and that he is in absolute ignorance of the King's intentions. They prattle much together, but there is no single point on which they have yet come to any stipulation. True it is that five days are scarcely yet elapsed. But wherefore presume?—— The Prince supports the minister, Schulemburg; and I know that Schulem-

---

leads us to suspect the truth of *such* an accusation. Still, his love for his dogs while living, his manner of treating them, and his last request to be buried by their side, are very strange, or, in a man like him, very whimsical facts. One of these favourites, a greyhound bitch, was taken at the battle of Sorr, when the baggage was plundered by Trenck and Nadasti. Regardless of inferior losses, the King was in the act of writing to Nadasti, to request his bitch might be restored, when the Austrian general, knowing his love for the animal, which was itself greatly attached to him, he sent it back; the bitch, unperceived by the Monarch, leaped upon the table while he was writing, and, as usual, began to caress him, at which he was so affected that he shed tears. The day before he had cut off many thousands of men, and charged his *dear children* to give no Saxon quarter.

burg found the King dry and cold. He had one choice for the French Embassy; and I know the King has another, which he has not even concealed from the Prince. The Monarch hears all, but is in nothing explicit. Bishopswerder himself perhaps does not know what he is to be, and, if he be prudent, will not be in too great haste.

I have twice seen Count Hertzberg, and found him still the same, a small portion of dissimulation excepted. He very positively denied being English. He does not seem to me to think he has the least need of Prince Henry, whom he has not been to visit (which is very marked, or rather indecent, behaviour) since his promotion to the order of the Black Eagle. I wished to insinuate to him that it would be easy to consult the uncle by the aid of the nephew; this he declined, but gave me an apologetic memorial for Prince Henry, relative to his personal discussions with Baron Knyphausen. Either Prince Henry or Hertzberg, or both, are much deceived. Hertzberg certainly sups almost every night with the King; and the opinion of some well-informed people is that this minister, and General Moellendorf, will be appointed to educate the Prince of Prussia.

The Marquis of Luchesini is continued in his place by the present King; but hitherto he has only been desired to write the poem for the funeral. The secretary of Prince Henry, it is said, is to compose the music; and this is one of the things which turn the uncle's brain.

I have sent the King my grand memorial[1]; he has only acknowledged having received it, adding that I might remain persuaded whatever should come from me would give him pleasure; and that, of all the obliging things that were said to him, none flattered him more highly than mine.

☼

P.S. — The ministers took the oath of allegiance yesterday, about three o'clock; hence, no probable changes for some time to come. Count Arnim Boytzemburg, sent for by the King, arrived with all haste, and passed the evening with His Majesty. I believe him proper for nothing but

---

[1] The memorial found at the end of the second volume.

a place about Court; it may, however, have relation to the embassy to France, but more probably to the place of grand marshal, or that of minister of the Landschafft, a kind of president of the provinces, who greatly influences the assessments of the taxes, and other internal arrangements.

LETTER XVII

August 26th, 1786.

I FEAR my prophecies will be accomplished. Prince Henry appears to me to have gained nothing but bows from his nephew. One article of the will of the King's grandfather disposed of the succession of certain bailliages, so as to bequeath an accession of income, of about forty or fifty thousand crowns, to Prince Henry; including an augmentation of the revenue of Prince Ferdinand. Circumstances not being exactly the same now as supposed by the testator, the ministers (that is to say, Hertzberg) have pretended that this bequest no longer was legal; and the King, eluding to grant the legacy, has made a proposal to his uncle to have the suit determined either in Germany, France or Italy. The Prince has written an ingenious and noble letter to him, but in which he indicates the enemy. The King has redoubled his outward caresses for his uncle, and has submitted to three judges, who have been nominated by the Prince. I hence conclude that the uncle will gain the suit of the bailliages, but never that of the regency.

Hertzberg, however, has commissioned me to make some advances from himself to the Prince, and this I think is a sign that he is not in perfect security. I never could prevail on the Prince to comply; sometimes inflated, sometimes agitated, he neither could command his countenance nor his first emotions. He is deceitful, yet knows not how to dissemble; endowed with ideas, wit, and even a portion of understanding, but has not a single opinion of his own. Petty means, petty councils, petty passions, petty prospects; all is diminutive in the soul of that man. While he makes gigantic pretensions, he has a mind without method; is as haughty as an upstart, and as vain as a man who had no claim to respect; he can neither lead nor be led. He is one of too frequent examples that insignificance of character may stifle the greatest qualities.

The thing the new King fears the most is being thought to be governed; and in this respect Prince Henry, of all men, is the least adapted to the Monarch; who I believe would consent not to reign, provided he might only be supposed to reign.

Remarkable change!—The general directory is restored to the footing on which it was under Frederick William I.[1] This is a wise act. The result of the madness of innovation, under Frederick II. was that, of all the Kings in Europe, he was the most deceived. The mania of expediting the whole affairs of a kingdom in one hour and a half, was the cause that the ministers were each of them absolute in their departments. At present, all must be determined in a committee; each will have occasion of the consent and sanction of all the rest. In a word, it is a kind of council. This, no doubt, will have its inconveniences; but how are inconveniences to be avoided?

The edict for suppressing the Lotto is signed, as I am assured. I shall at least have done this much good to the country.[2]—But the King has permitted the last drawing, which is wrong;

---

[1] The predecessor of the late King.
[2] See the before-mentioned memorial.

there ought to have been none under his reign. Perhaps it is only popular report.

The Duke of Brunswick arrived this evening. M. Ardenberg-Reventlau, a man of merit and his favourite minister—(though M. Feronce is the principal)—preceded him, and was here at a quarter after four. The Duke was admitted to see his Majesty, who rises at four o'clock; at half after six he was on the parade. The King received him neither with distance nor ardour. Perhaps nothing more is meant by this journey than politeness. Necessity only could make such a man prime minister, who will not trouble himself with fruitless efforts, but who will be very tenacious in his grasp. I shall not converse with him till to-morrow. The will he brings will probably be burnt; it is said to be of a much earlier date than the other, and as far back as 1755.

The Landgrave of Hesse-Cassel, it is affirmed, is coming; also the Duke of Weymar, the Prince of Deux-Ponts, and even the Duke of York. Of the latter I doubt.

Hertzberg pretends that the King, by becoming

the pledge of the Stadtholder, ought to make us easy concerning Holland, but he has not told us who shall make the pledge respected.

Prince Henry wishes advice should be sent that Count Hertzberg, who has not the good word of all the world, appears to have gained the entire confidence of the King, and even to act the master. This last imputation is probably the most effectual method to procure the downfall of any man, under the present reign.

There are many small Court favours granted, but no considerable place bestowed. I have attempted to reconcile Hertzberg and Knyphausen, which I was in a train to accomplish, by demonstrating to them that their coalition would erect a throne which could not be shaken. Knyphausen refused, because, alleged he, Hertzberg is so deceitful it can never be known whether the reconciliation is or is not sincere; "and it is better," said the Baron, "to be the open enemy than the equivocal friend of a man whose credit is superior to our own."

I am inclined to think Hertzberg must be displaced, if we wish the Prussians should become

French. Three months are necessary to draw any conclusions that should be at all reasonable. I again repeat, if you have any grand political views, relative to this country and Germany, put an end to the democratical quarrels of Holland; which are only the disputes of cunning, profitable to those who have their fortunes to make, but not to those whose fortunes are made.

LETTER XVIII

August 29th, 1786.

To prophesy here daily becomes more difficult; time only can afford any rational prognostics. The King apparently intends to renounce all his old habits; this is a proud undertaking. He has made three visits to Schoenhausen,[1] nor has he cast one look on Mademoiselle Voss: no semblance of an Orgia; not one woman's bosom touched since he has sate on the throne. One of his confidants proposed a visit to Charlottenburg. —"No," replied he; "all my former allurements are there."—He retires before ten in the evening, and rises at four; he works excessively, and certainly with some difficulty. Should he persevere, he will afford a singular example of habits of thirty years being vanquished. This will be an indubitable proof of a grand character, and shew how we have all been mistaken. But even, the supposition granted, which is so far from probable,

---

[1] The Queen's palace.

how deficient are his understanding and his means. I say how deficient, since even his most ecstatic panegyrists begin by giving up his understanding. The last day that he exercised the troops, he was ridiculously slow, heavy, and monotonous. The men were four times ranged in columns, and concluded with parading. This continued three hours; and in the presence of a general such as is the Duke of Brunswick.—Everybody was dissatisfied.—Yesterday, the first Court day, he was ill; he forgot some of the foreign ministers, and uttered nothing but a few commonplace phrases, hasty, embarrassed, and ill-chosen; this scarcely continued five minutes. He immediately left us to go to church: for he does not miss church; and religious zeal, homilies and pulpit flatteries already begin to be everywhere heard and seen.

Prince Henry has gained his suit, concerning the bailliages, as I had foreseen; in other respects, he has not advanced a step; consequently, has gone backward. He dines every day with the King, and does wrong; he affects to whisper with him, and does wrong; he speaks to him of public affairs incessantly, and does wrong. The King goes alone to visit the Duke of Brunswick; and also goes in company with Hertzberg, or meets him at the Duke's. The latter pretends to interfere only with the army; the sole thing which, according to him, he understands. I have never yet seen him in private, but he has appointed me an audience on Wednesday morning.

The English faction continues very active, and this proves there are difficulties to encounter. In reality, it is an alliance so unnatural, when compared to ours, that it seems to me we should not suffer ourselves, though the King should commit blunders, to be routed by his mistakes.

The Monarch becomes very difficult effectually to observe. He reverts to the severe ceremonies of German etiquette. It is imagined he will not receive foreigners, at least for some time. I know all that can be learnt from subaltern spies; from valets, courtiers, secretaries, and the intemperate tongue of Prince Henry; but there are only two modes of influencing; which are to give, or rather to give birth to, ideas in the master, or in his ministers. In the master!—How, since he is not to be approached? In the ministers!—It is neither very easy nor very prudent to speak to them on public affairs, I not being in a public character; and the discussions which chance affords are short, vague and incomplete. If I am supposed capable of business, I ought to be sent to some place where I should have a public character. I am afraid I shall here cost more than I am worth.

Count Goertz goes to Holland; I know not whether instead of Thulemeyer or *ad tempus*. He is followed by the son of Count Arnim, who is a young shoot for the corps diplomatique. Goertz is not a man without talents: when sent into Russia, under every kind of disadvantage, he obtained a good knowledge of the country; he is cold, dry and ungracious; but subtle, master of his temper, though violent, and a man of observation. That he is of the English party is certain; he is loyal to Hertzberg, and convinced that the alliance of Holland and France is so unnatural it must soon end. I own I think as he does, especially should we abuse our power.

A new ambassador is appointed, *in petto*, for France. I have not yet been able to discover who; but Hertzberg supports the ridiculous Goltz with all his power. Schulemburg daily declines in favour. The maritime company have already lost their monopoly of coffee, of which there are four millions and a half pounds, weight consumed in the various provinces of the Prussian monarchy. Hence we may observe that the free use of coffee, which daily becomes general in Germany, is the cause that the consumption of beer is gradually and much less. The same company may be deprived of a prodigious profit on sugars; but it will be in vain to destroy old monopolies only to substitute new, though they should be for the profit of the King.

The personal debts of his Majesty are paying off by the minister, Blumenthal; it is said there are tolerably great reductions made, but not unjustly, as I imagine, for there are no complaints on the subject. Exclusive of the royal treasury, Frederick II. has left savings so great that they will scarcely be absorbed by the personal debts of Frederick William II. It is said he will pay off his Italian opera, and everybody believes there will be a French opera instead. This certainly would be no trifling means of support to intrigue.

The freedom of scrutiny is restored to the academy, and the Germans are henceforward to be admitted members. I regard the curatorship of this body as a favour conferred on, and a tolerable resource of power for Hertzberg; who will be curator by title, and president in reality. The presidency of the academy is so truly ministerial that the late Frederick exercised it himself, after the decease of the restless and morose Maupertuis. Count Hertzberg said to me, at Court—"You are a compliment in my debt."—"On what occasion?"—"I am curator of the academy; which title gives me greater pleasure, and in my opinion is more honorable than a ribband."—Forty persons heard our discourse.— "Certainly," replied I, "he who is the minister of knowledge may well be called the prime minister."

The King will not ruin himself in gifts; he has hitherto bestowed only prebendaries, which cost him nothing, except a pension of three hundred crowns on General Levald. I am informed that he has just granted one of eight hundred crowns—to the poet Rammler. It would perhaps have been more delicate not to have begun by pensioning fame, and her trumpet.

LETTER XIX

September 2nd, 1786.

ALL circumstances confirm my predictions. Prince Henry and his nephew have almost quarrelled. The uncle is inconsolable, and thinks of retiring to Rheinsberg. He will almost certainly return during the journey of the King through Prussia and Silesia. Probably we shall have no great changes before the Monarch has performed these journeys, if then. There is one, however, beside those I have before spoken of, which is remarkable; and that is, a commission to examine the administration of the customs—what is to be abrogated, what preserved, and what qualified, especially in the excise.

M. Werder, a minister of state, and the intimate friend of Hertzberg, the enemy of Schulemburg who brought him into place, and father-in-law to the secretary of the English Embassy, or perhaps to his wife, is at the head of this commission. The other members are ridiculously selected; but the very project of such a reform is most agreeable to the nation; as much so as the pension of eight hundred crowns granted to the poet Rammler, and the promise of admission of Germans into the academy is to the distributors of renown. It remains to be seen whether the people have not been led to hope too much; and whether it is not requisite to be certain of substitutes, previous to the promise of relief.

The King goes to Prussia attended by Messieurs Hertzberg (for the King to be attended by a minister out of his department is unexampled), Goltz, surnamed the Tartar, Boulet, a French engineer, General Goertz, Gaudi, and Bishopswerder.

This Goltz the Tartar is he who, in the last campaign of the seven years' war, raised an insurrection of fifty thousand Tartars, in the Crimea and the neighbouring countries; who were marching to make a diversion in favour of the King of Prussia, and had arrived at Bender, when peace was concluded. Notwithstanding this, Goltz can boast of but little abilities; except that he is a good officer, and ardently active.

He was indebted for his great and singular success to a Dutchman named Biskamp, whom he met with in the Crimea. He attached himself to this very able and enterprizing man, who understood the language, knew the country, and served Frederick II. according to his wishes; by whom, indeed, he was well paid. This Biskamp is at Warsaw, and there forgotten, which is very strange. I have supposed the relating this anecdote, which is but little known, might be interesting.

Boulet is an honest man, for whom the King shews some affection, and to whom he is indebted for all he knows concerning fortification.

General Goertz is the brother of the Goertz who is going to Holland, but not his equal; he is artful and subtle, and his good faith is of a suspicious complexion.

Gaudi is the brother of the celebrated general of the same name; little known hitherto as the minister of the Prussian department, but capable, well-informed, firm, decided, and indubitably the man most proper to influence interior arrangements in reconstructing the grand directory.

Bishopswerder you are acquainted with; he and Boulet each lately received the commission of lieutenant-colonel.

The King has told Schulemburg that, on his return from Prussia, he will determine which of his nine departments he shall be deprived of. He and his wife are the only ministerial family who are not invited to Court. The probabilities all are that Schulemburg will demand leave to resign, should his colleagues continue to humble him, and the King to treat him with contempt. But Struensee probably will keep his place, and he then proposes to act, in concert with us, in our public funds; especially should the King, as is apparent, commit to his charge the four millions of crowns (about sixteen millions of French livres, or near seven hundred thousand pounds sterling) which he means to set apart, for the operations of previous finance. Struensee is the only man who understands them. This is a subject not to be neglected, as it hitherto has been, even so far as to render it impossible for me to act with propriety. We might profit by him, during peace; but if unfortunately the news which is whispered be true, concerning the increasing ill-health of the Elector of Bavaria, depend upon war, for I then hold it inevitable. Is this a time for us to exist from day to day, as we do, when each month (for there is a probability, at any time, that he should die within a month) menaces all Europe with inextricable confusion?

M. de Larrey, sent from the Stadtholder to compliment the King, openly affirms it is impossible the disputes of Holland should be appeased without effusion of blood; and the speculations of Hertzberg upon this subject are boundless; but the secret is well kept by those who surround the King.

LETTER XX

TO THE DUKE DE ———

September 2nd, 1786.

BY what fatality, my Lord, has it happened that I have not received your letter, dated the sixteenth, till this day? And, still more especially, why was it not written some weeks sooner? The importance of the proposition with which it concludes will never be fully understood; and which, made at any other time, except when the King was dying, would have been willingly accepted. It will never be known, had it been presented soon enough, how much it might have effected, impeded and indicated, relative to a Prince whose understanding perhaps is not great, but who possesses gratitude, and who will much more certainly be an honest man than a great King; so that his heart, rather than his mind, ought to have been appealed to; and that at a time when he was far otherwise accessible than at present; walled in, as he is, by system and intrigue. How does it happen that you are the only person of the country you inhabit who conceived this plan? How could the Cabinet of Versailles give up the merit of offering trifling sums to Serilly? How could it permit the Duke of Courland to secure the claim of having hushed the loud cries of creditors to silence? How impolitic and disastrous are the sordid views, the confined plans, and short-sighted prudence of certain persons! In what a situation would such an act have placed us, as it would me personally, in his opinion! All things then would have been possible, would have been easy to me. But of this we must think no more; we must only remember this is a new proof that reason is always on your side.

Since the death of the King I have sent supplies of information to your Cabinet, respecting the *Aulic phases*,[1] and my dispatch of to-day, a great part of which no doubt our common friend will read to you, is a statement, according to the best of my abilities, of present and future contingencies. You will there perceive Prince Henry has accomplished his own destiny; that his trifling

---

[1] Court changes, or appearances.

character has, on this occasion, weighty as it was, been stranded on the rock of his excessive vanity, as it has before so often been; that he has at once displayed an excessive desire of power, disgusting haughtiness, insupportable pedantry, and a disdain of intrigue, at the same time that his conduct was one continuation of petty, low, dirty cabal; that he has despised the people in power, while he himself is surrounded by no creature who is not evidently either foolish, knavish or contemptible—one sole man, Baron Knyphausen, excepted—and he is in daily danger of being carried off by apoplexy; that, in fine, no man can be more out of favour, and particularly of confidence, or can have put himself into a situation in which confidence and favour will be more difficult to regain.

I therefore persist in my opinion that the Duke of Brunswick, who is master of himself, by no means ostentatious, and who is possessed of profound talents, will be the man; not of the present moment, but of the moment of necessity. My reasons are numerous, and so deduced as, in my opinion, not to admit of contradiction, the order of events and circumstances, which I see and foresee considered. All this does but render the execution of your project the more necessary, and which I regard as very practicable, with some small exceptions, if executed by the persons in whom you ought to confide; should you, with your natural dexterity, and irresistible seduction, pursue the plan of interesting the vanity of the MASTER, so as to make it his own act, and, as you have so well expressed it, that it shall be he himself who shall inform his ministers of his intentions.

I repeat, your project is the more immediately necessary because that England cabals, with great industry, in her own behalf, under the pretence of the interests of Holland, which are very much at heart, in the Cabinet of Berlin. I own that what I have often insinuated here, namely, that the Prussian power is not sufficiently consolidated, and that, if opposed to stand the shock of France and Austria combined, it must be reduced to powder, is a proposition not so unanswerable, but that, thanks to Russia, there are many objections to be made; and so there always will be, even in suppositions the most unfavourable to Prussia.

1. Because this would but be commencing a deplorable career of sanguinary contentions, under the direction of the Emperor, who is so little able to direct that he may be affirmed to be the least military of men.

2. That the utmost success would leave a Prince without counterpoise in Europe, who has claims and pretensions of every kind.

Lastly, and more especially, this would be painfully to seek that which the nature of events spontaneously offers ; like as spring makes the apparently dry and sapless tree bud and bloom.

There are some errors in cyphering, which are the cause that I do not perfectly understand the grounds of your dissension with me, concerning the maritime system ; but I too well know the extreme justness of your mind, which does not remain satisfied with phantoms, to imagine our opinions are very opposite. And, for my own part, I have never pretended to say that we ought not to maintain a navy which should make our commerce respected. The question to determine is—What ought the extent of this commerce to be, which is to be effectually protected? You, like me, perceive that no alliance with England can be solidly established but by a commercial treaty, which should have exact, clear and distinct lines of demarcation; for, were unlimited freedom of trade permitted, they would be the sufferers. How might they support the rivalship? And, if we do not cut away the voracious suckers from the root of the tree, how shall we prevent the Indies and Antilles from eternally continuing the apple of discord?

Be this as it may, my Lord, do not suffer yourself to be discouraged or disgusted by difficulties. Ascend the height with a firm though measured step, and with inflexible constancy. You have found the only unbeaten track which, in these times, can lead to political fame, and which best may tend to the pacification of the earth. How admirable is it to unite the talents of the hero, the principles of the sage, and the projects of the philosopher! By a single diplomatic act to reverse all the obsolete forms, all pitiable rubrics, all the destructive arts of modern politics, would be to gain no vulgar crown; and a prospect so magnificent must be a most powerful support to your fortitude.

I need not repeat how much I am devoted to you, or how entirely you may dispose of me.

LETTER XXI

September 5th, 1786.

IT is impossible that I should send you intelligence more exact, concerning the situation of Prince Henry with the King, than that which my preceding letters contain. The Prince himself no longer conceals the truth; and, like all weak men, passing from one extreme to the other, he clamourously affirms the country is undone; that priests, blockheads, prostitutes, and Englishmen are hastening its destruction; and, by the intemperance of his language, confirms what the indiscretion of Chevalier d'Oraison, and the personal confidence of the uncle to the nephew, when he was only Prince of Prussia, probably before but too certainly told Frederick William II. I repeat, he has completed his disgrace, in the private estimation of the King. It is my opinion that, if he may be permitted, he will either quit this country, in which he has not one friend, one parasite, except in the most subaltern and abject class, or will become insane, or will die: such is my augury.

Not that I am convinced that the administration must always be committed to subalterns. The King has too much dread of seeming to be governed not to have the necessity of being governed. Why should he be the first man who should pretend to be what he is not? Frederick II., who by nature was so perfectly designed to govern, never testified a fear of being governed; he was certain of the contrary. The present King fears he shall, and therefore shall be. While public affairs are transacted separately, he will not seem to be; for nothing is more easy in this country than to receive and to pay. The machinery is so wound up that the surplus of revenue is great indeed. It is easy to pay some attention to detail, to keep watch over the police, to make some subordinate changes, and to coquet with the nation. And here be it said, by the way, there seems a determination of humbling the vanity of foreigners; so that, as I have always affirmed, the *gallomania*[1] of Prince Henry has been very prejudicial to us. Some good will

---

[1] Enthusiasm in favour of France.

be done; for it is not here as in other kingdoms, where the passing from evil to good is sometimes worse than evil itself, and where there is terror in resistance. All is here done *ad nutum*. Beside, the cords are so stretched they cannot but relax: the people have been so oppressed, have suffered such vexation, such extortion, that they must find ease. All will proceed, therefore, and almost without aid, while foreign politics shall continue calm and uniform; but, whenever a gun is fired, or even at the first lowering storm, with what a petty crash will this scaffolding of mediocrity come to the ground! How will these subaltern ministers shrink; from the slave at the oar to the terrified steersman? How will they call for a pilot's aid?

Who must be this pilot? — The Duke of Brunswick. Of this I have no doubt. Every little accident, in the day of trouble, is only an additional aptitude to fear. Beside that the Prince is, of all men, him who best can conduct little vanity: he will satisfy himself with appearing the servant of servants; the most polite, the most humble, and indubitably the most adroit of courtiers; while, at the same time, his iron hand will fetter all paltry views, all trifling intrigues, all inferior factions. Such is the horoscope I draw; nor do I think, at present, one more rational can be erected.

Hertzberg is the man who must be managed in the state; and for this Count d'Esterno is not qualified, because he formerly deserted him too much; and he well perceived it would have been indelicate and stupid to have veered too suddenly. Hertzberg, however, may ruin himself by his boasting, and even by his ostentation. This is a mode of effecting the fall of ministers which the courtiers will not fail to employ, because of the character of the King, and which may succeed.

But Holland and her convulsions are the subject of present consideration. There is a conviction that we can do what we please; and, though I am far from thinking this to be incontrovertible, I still think that, were we to say to the party that has gained so much ground, probably from a conviction that we were ready to march up to their support—(For how would

they have dared to make themselves responsible,
if they had possessed no securities for such
future contingencies as may be expected?)—I
repeat, were we to say, *you must go no further*,
we should be obeyed. It will be supposed, I
neither pretend nor wish to give advice. I am
too far removed from truth, which I can only
inspect through the magnifying glass of passion;
and Count d'Esterno informs me of nothing:
but I can distinctly perceive that the hurricane,
which is forming in those marshes, may extend
to other countries. The French Embassy of
Berlin will not say thus much to you, because
they do not see things in the same light, but
are persuaded that the interest of the brother
will have no influence on the connections of the
King. Of this I doubt, and have good reason
so to doubt. Hertzberg is wholly Dutch, for it
is the only decent manner in which he can be
English; and he may greatly influence foreign
politics, although he does not understand them.
As, the other day, he was rehearsing his eternal
repetition of — THE KING WILL BE THE PLEDGE
OF THE STADTHOLDER—I said to him, "I respect

the King too much to ask who shall be the pledge of the pledge; but I dare venture to ask — *How will the King make his pledge respected?* What shall happen when France shall demonstrate that the Stadtholder has broken engagements entered into under her sanction? The King is not the brother-in-law of Holland; and the affair of Naples is sufficient proof that family interventions may be eluded? What can the King accomplish against Holland? And is he not too equitable to require us, who cannot wish that the Dutch should become English, to risk our alliance for the knight-errant of the English?" — To all this Hertzberg, who beholds nothing on this sublunary earth but HERTZBERG and PRUSSIA, made vague replies; but, at the words, "What can the King accomplish against Holland?" he muttered, with a gloomy air, "*Holland will not defy him, I believe.*" Once again, beware of Holland; where, by way of parenthesis, the English legation affirms that we have bought the town of Schiedam; that M. de Calonne, in particular, inundates the country with gold; and, in a word, that he is personally the brand of discord.

I have reserved the questions with which your letter begins, to conclude with; first, because they relate to affairs the least pressing; since it appears impossible that the Emperor should make any attempts on Turkey in Europe before the coming spring; and next, it was necessary I should previously recollect myself; the concurring circumstances of the death of the King, and the accession of Frederick William, being the subjects which have almost exclusively demanded my attention, and induced me to defer more distant objects to future consideration. Still, I fear mine is a barren harvest, Prussia not having any continued intercourse with these wide lying countries, which are more than four hundred leagues distant; for she has neither any great merchant, nor any system of politics, because that the corps diplomatique of Prussia is extremely deficient.

As to those individuals that are met with in society, they are ignorant, and can afford no information. Buckholz, the Prussian envoy to Warsaw, a man of ordinary capacity, but active, and Huttel, who is in the same capacity at Petersburg, an intelligent person, write word that

Russia is more pacific than Turkey; and that the internal Ottoman provinces call for war. The frontier provinces, appertaining to the Tartars, certainly are not friendly to Russia. Moldavia and Wallachia are governed by Hospodars, who, being Greeks, most certainly are sold to whoever will purchase them, consequently to Russia. The Emperor deceives them, and is hated there, as elsewhere. I shall speak further of this, and shall endeavour to give a sketch of a journey along the frontiers of these countries, which should be undertaken in the disguise of a trader, and kept rigidly secret, by which the state of the frontiers, the magazines, the propensities of the people, &c., &c., might be known, and what is to be hoped or feared, if it be found necessary to arm (in which case it is very probable Prussia would voluntarily aid us with all her powers); that is to say, if the Emperor should determine to pay no respect to our remonstrances, as he has twice done before.

Perhaps I might be more useful employed in such a journey than at Berlin, where at every step I tread on danger, and shall so continue to do, unless I have credentials, at least as an assistant;

which perhaps would be the more proper, because it sometimes happens that such an interlocutor is spoken to with greater freedom than an ambassador; for the refusals he meets, or the proposals he makes, have no ministerial consequences; and thus each party gains information, without either being offended.

Pay serious attention to this, I request. In vain you recommend me to act privately; permit me to inform you that, in despite of all my efforts, this is impracticable. I have too much celebrity, too much intercourse with Prince Henry, who is a true Joan of Arc, and who has no secrets of any kind. I am made to speak when I am silent; and when I say anything it is unfaithfully repeated. It is impossible to conceive all that has been attributed to me since the King's death; that is to say, since an epocha when I have taken advantage of the interruption of social meetings to keep myself recluse, and to labour only by mining. Count d'Esterno discredits me all in his power. The English Embassy exclaims "*Fœnum habet in cornu, longè fuge.*" The favourites keep me at a distance; the wits, the priests, and the mystics have formed a league, &c., &c. Each fears an invasion of his domains, because my real business is not known. I cannot remain and be of any utility, unless you shall find means to inform Count Finckenstein that I am only a good citizen and a good observer; but that these I am, and that I am authorized to give my opinion. I cannot doubt but that this minister is very desirous these few words should be said. I am, however, in conscience obliged to repeat, the part I have to play daily becomes more difficult and more invidious; and that, in order to be truly useful, I must have some character given me, or be employed elsewhere.

Prince Henry at present reads his recantation; he again pretends Hertzberg has received his death-blow, and that his downfall will be instantaneous. He relates miracles of the Duke of Brunswick, and flatters himself he shall, soon or late, have great influence—" He will be in no haste. He will ply to windward six months." He affirms the English projects are absolutely abortive. Hertzberg, he is confident, acts as if he had lost all understanding, and precisely as if he, Prince

Henry, had counselled him, in order to render his fall more headlong, &c., &c., &c. In fine, his discourse is a mixture of enthusiasm and rhodomontade, of presumption and anxiety; a flux of words that confirm nothing; or of half-phrases without any determinate meaning, except of exaggeration and tumour. Hence, it is difficult to conjecture whether he deceives himself or wishes to deceive; whether he maintains the cause of vanity, feasts on illusion, or if he has recently any ray of hope; for, as I have said, it is not impossible but that Hertzberg, by his boasting, should effect his own ruin. Prince Henry presses me to request the Court to send me some credentials, while the King shall be in Prussia and Silesia; or, at least, to write concerning me to Count Finckenstein, by whom the intelligence may be communicated to the King.

No change in the new habits of the Monarch. Madam Rietz has been but once to see him; but, on Saturday last, he wrote to his natural son by that woman, and directed his letter: "To my son, Alexander Count de la Marche.[1]" He has

---

[1] Meaning one of the Marches of Brandenburg.

ennobled, and even made a Baroness of the mistress of the Margrave of Schwedt (Baroness of Stoltzenberg, which is the title of a Barony, worth about eight thousand crowns a year, given her by the Margrave), who is nothing more than a tolerably pretty German girl, formerly an actress, by whom the Margrave has a son. It was not thought proper to refuse the only thing this old Prince of seventy-seven wished to or could request. Perhaps, too, it was a pretext to do as much for Madam Rietz. The husband of this lady is Erzkaemmerer,[1] a place nearly corresponding to that of first valet-de-chambre, and treasurer of the privy purse; but it is supposed he will do nothing more than get rich; his wife hitherto has never had any serious influence.

The Court marshal, Ritwitz, having suddenly become raving mad, after a quarrel with one of the provision officers, Marwitz, who is a totally insignificant person, has been proposed to the King. "He will do as well as another," replied the Monarch. Is this thoughtlessness, or is it fear of importance being annexed to a place

---

[1] Arch-Chamberlain.

which in reality but little merits importance? This question it is impossible to answer.

Lucchesini increases in his pretensions; he demands a place in the finance or commercial department; perhaps the direction of the Maritime Company, but this would be a very lofty stride. Annexed to wit and information, he has some qualities to which ambition is seldom allied; at most they will entitle him to become a member of the corps diplomatique, of which he is capable. I believe this Italian to be one of the most ardent in keeping me at a distance from the King, who will not indeed be easy of access before the winter.

The commission of regulations has hitherto rather appeared a caustic than a healing and paternal remedy. There is much more talk of the sums, the employment of which cannot be justified, than of easing the excise. Verder, the president, is beside known to be the personal enemy of some of the members of the tax administration. This, perhaps, has occasioned suspicions. Verder, however, was proposed by the Duke of Brunswick, who, in fact, had need of his aid in some affairs that relate to his country.

Hertzberg has certainly been in a storm, and the credit of Count Finckenstein appears to be augmented, though I confess the shade of increasing favour is scarcely perceptible. I persist in believing that Hertzberg is immovable, unless by his want of address.

LETTER XXII

September 8th, 1786.

The sixth, at a review of the artillery, I dismounted my horse to attend the King, in the front of the ranks. The Duke of Brunswick joined me; and, as we talked of mortars, bombs and batteries, we gradually removed to a distance. As soon as we were alone, he began to speak to me of the prodigious knowledge I had of the country; giving me to understand he had read my memorial to the King. He then reverted to the new reign; and suddenly afterward to foreign politics. Having entered at length into the subject, and spoken more than is necessary here to repeat, he added —" In God's name, arrange affairs in Holland; free the King of his fears. Must the Stadtholder never be other than *ad honores?* You are in full credit there, and this credit you cannot lose; if you did, the party by which you obtained it would be too much exposed to danger. I repeat, put us at our ease, and I will answer on my head for everything else : but use despatch, I conjure you. On Sunday I shall depart for Brunswick; come and visit me, while the King is gone into Silesia; we can converse freely there, and nowhere else. But write to your friends that they ought to exert all their influence to engage the French ministry to use moderation with the Prince of Orange, who cannot be proscribed without state convulsions. Things are not ripe for his abolishment; give him protection. France cannot render a greater service to Europe. What, is your Court yet to learn those forms which effect no change, but which give every support?" Here we separated, because the subject began to be too interesting. But tell me — ought I not to go to Brunswick?

To this I should add that Count Goertz has taken eight chasseurs with him, who are to convey letters to the frontiers of the Prussian states, in order that no despatches may be sent by land, nor pass through foreign hands. The Duke of Brunswick has repeated what Prince Henry had told me, and which I forgot to inform you of, that one of the principal motives for selecting Count Goertz was his former friendship with M. de Veyrac.

From my conversation with the Duke, I conclude that he is or soon will be master of affairs; and this explains the new fit of joy, hope, and presumption which has seized on Prince Henry, who has been persuaded by the cunning Duke that, if he will but have patience, the sceptre will devolve on him; and that he, the Duke, will be no more than high constable. It is said Koenigsberg will be appointed field-marshal. This, added to the smooth turn which the Duke has given discussions and pecuniary matters, has turned the Prince's brain, who told me the other day—"That the Duke was the most loyal of men, and his best friend; that he owned a fortnight ago he was of a different opinion; but that, &c." So that the metamorphosis has been produced within this fortnight. In truth, there is no real difference between a fool and a man of understanding, who thus can suffer himself to be deceived; as little is there between a fool and a man of understanding, who can be persuaded that a fool is a man of understanding. Both these things daily happen to Prince Henry. On the thirteenth he departs for Rheinsberg and is to return the day before the King.

The fervour of the novice appears somewhat

to abate. I have good reason to believe that Mademoiselle Voss is ready to capitulate. Ogling, frequent conversations (for the present assiduity at Schoenhausen is not paid to the Queen Dowager), presents accepted (a canonicate for her brother), and an attempt at influence. (It is she who placed Mademoiselle Vierey in the service of the Princess Frederica of Prussia.) To ask is to grant. Since the accession all circumstances denote how dazzling is the lustre of a diadem; but so much the better, for her fall only can render her but little dangerous. She is wholly English, and is not incapable of intrigue. When we reflect that the credit of a Madam du Troussel had the power, under a Frederick II., to bestow places of importance, we may imagine what may happen under another King, as soon as it shall be discovered that intrigue may be employed at the Court of Berlin, as well as at other Courts.

Madam Rietz yesterday received a diamond worth four thousand crowns: she will probably be put on the invalid list, with some money, and perhaps a title.

Her son, at present, has publicly the title of

Count de la Marche (or Count Brandenburg), and has a separate establishment.

General Kalckstein, disgraced by the late King, and regretted by everybody, has received a regiment.

At present, and till I hear other news relative to Berlin, accept the following important anecdote; and which I think it necessary to send in the now doubtful state of the health of the Empress of Russia.—About six years ago a young foreigner, and a gentleman, in the service of France, was presented to the Grand-Duchess, by a lady who had been educated with her, and who has remained her intimate friend. It was the intention of this young gentleman to enter into the Russian service: he was presented to the Grand Duke by the Grand-Duchess, who warmly solicited, and while he was present, a place for the youth in service of her husband.

The young favourite, well-formed and handsome, often visited the Grand-Duchess. Invited to her palace, feasted, distinguished, and continually receiving new favours, he fell in love; of which the Grand-Duchess was informed by his extreme confusion. One grand Court-day, at a masked ball, in the evening, she had him conducted by one of her women into an obscure apartment, and sufficiently distant from those where the Court was held. In a little time the conductress quitted him, and advised him to wait; and the Grand-Duchess arrived in a black domino. She removed her mask, took the youth by the hand, led him to a sofa, and made him sit down by her side. The Grand-Duchess then told him this was the moment for him to choose between the service of France and the service of Russia. A certain time, however, was allowed him to come to a decision. Coquetry and even caresses succeeded. Wavering, taken by surprise, distracted between love and fear, the youth behaved with excessive awkwardness at the beginning of the interview. The Grand-Duchess, however, encouraged him, inspired him with audacity, and made him every advance, till at length he vanquished his timidity, and indeed became very daring.

To this scene of transports, adieus suddenly succeeded, which partook as much of terror, and of despotism, as of love. The Grand-Duchess commanded the youth, in the most tender but the most absolute tone, to inform the Grand Duke that he could not accept the rank of captain, which was intended to be given him. She added that he must depart, instantly depart; and that his head must answer should the least circumstance transpire. She at the same time pressed him to demand some mark of remembrance. The terrified youth, confused and trembling, requested a black ribband, which she took from her domino. He received the pledge, and so totally lost all recollection, that he left the ball, and quitted Petersburg, without contriving any means of correspondence, arrangements for the future, or precautions of any kind, in favour of his fortune. In a few days he left Russia, travelling day and night, and did not write to the Grand Duke till he had passed the frontiers. He received a very gracious answer; and here the affair ended.

This person is returned to, and is now in, the service of France. He has little firmness, but does not want understanding. Were he guided he might certainly be useful; at least, attempts might be made after so extraordinary an accident. But for this it would be necessary he should go to

Russia before there is any change of Monarch, and should tempt his fortune, now that the Grand-Duchess has not so much fear. I am not personally acquainted with him, but I can dispose of his most intimate friend, in whom every dependence may be placed. I have not thought proper to name the hero of the romance, whom it is not necessary to know, unless it should be intended to afford him employment. If, on the contrary, it should be thought proper for him to pursue any such plan, I will name him instantly.

The Elector of Bavaria is certainly not in good health; he may not live to see winter; and it is scarcely probable he will reach the spring. I shall go from hence to Dresden, that I may not appear to absent myself purposely for the Duke of Brunswick. I shall remain there seven or eight days, as long at Brunswick, and three or four weeks in the whole. My journey will be exactly of the same duration as that of the King, in whose absence there is nothing to be learnt, and I shall certainly profit by my peregrinations, and learn more at Brunswick in a week than I should here divine in three months.

My letter is too long to speak of Turkey in Europe. I doubt the Emperor cannot be prevented, if he is not destitute of all capacity, of marching any day he shall please to the mouth of the Danube; but on the same day he must become the natural enemy of Russia, who will find in his presence one too many on the Black Sea, and this may render the combined projects abortive. I am assured that Moldavia and Wallachia desire to be under the Emperor's government. This I cannot believe, since his own peasants fly their country, and even go to Poland, rather than remain in his power. But the before mentioned provinces are absolutely unprotected, and I think no opposition can be made, except in Roumelia and Bulgaria. In fine, I believe we only, by promises or threats, are able to prevent the Emperor from labouring at this grand demolition. If we believe the rhodomontadoes of Petersburg, Russia is singly capable of the work. But, were she to attempt it, what would she be on the succeeding day? You are not ignorant she has received some check; that Prince Heraclius has been obliged to desert her cause; that she is once again reduced to defend Mount Caucasus as a frontier; that she cannot at present march into the heart of the Ottoman territories; and that perhaps this would be the best moment for recovering the Crimea. Should all these particulars be true, and these conjectures well founded, it is impossible that I should know any one of them so perfectly as you do yourself.

The dispute, relative to the bailliage of Wusterhausen, has been very nobly ended by the King. He has retaken it, but has made an annual grant of fifty thousand crowns to Prince Henry; seventeen thousand of which the latter is obliged to pay to Prince Ferdinand. The bailliage does not produce more than about forty-three thousand.

Prince Ferdinand at present recants the renunciation to the Margraviate of Anspach. As it is known that Prince Ferdinand has no will of his own, it is evident he receives his impulse from Prince Henry, and the more so, because this is the *manet altá mente repostum* against Count Hertzberg. It would be difficult to imagine anything more silly, or better calculated eternally to embroil him with the King.

I have always regarded the singularity of Romanzow, of not going into mourning, and his violence with Count Finckenstein concerning not sending a complimentary envoy to Petersburg, which occasioned the Count to demand whether he had orders from his Court to speak in such a style, as the effervescence of a young man; especially since Baron Reeden, the Dutch envoy, did not likewise go into mourning from economy, which shews it was not considered as a matter of any great importance. As these debates very ridiculously occupied the corps diplomatique for a week; and as the Count d'Esterno, who has conducted himself well on the occasion, must have mentioned it, I thought it to no purpose to write on the subject. But as Romanzow, of all the foreign ambassadors, did not attend the funeral at Potsdam, this mark, either of thoughtlessness or dissatisfaction, was felt; and, the time necessary to receive orders being past, I send information of the fact, to which I do not, however, pay so much attention as the good people in the pit, though it has greatly displeased the boxes. The Cabinet of Berlin must long have known that friendship, on the part of Russia, is hopeless till the accession of the Grand Duke; but it is impossible to butt with more force, or greater disrespect, than Romanzow has done.

LETTER XXIII

September 10th, 1786.

THE following are some particulars concerning what happened, on the day of interment, at Potsdam.

The King arrived at seven o'clock. At half-past seven he went with the Princesses Frederica and Louisa of Brunswick, the young ladies Knisbec, Voss, &c., to see the chamber of Frederick. It was small, hung with violet-coloured cloth, and loaded with ornaments of black and silver. At the far end was an alcove, on which the coffin was placed, under the portrait of the hero. This coffin was richly ornamented with cloth of silver, laced with gold. Toward the head was a casque of gold, the sword that Frederick wore, his military staff, the ribband of the Black Eagle, and gold spurs. Round the coffin were eight stools, on which were placed eight golden cushions, meant to sustain:—

1. The crown.
2. The golden globe and cross.
3. The gold box containing the seal.

4. The electoral cap.

5. The sceptre.

6. The order of the Golden Eagle, of diamonds and other precious stones.

7. The royal sword.

8. The royal hand.

The balustrade was hung with violet-coloured velvet. A splendid glass chandelier was in the centre, and on each side was a mutilated pyramid of white marble veined with black; that is to say, of white cloth, marbled with great art. The chamber appeared to me to want light.

His Majesty afterwards passed into the canopy saloon, hung with black, and adorned with plates of silver from the Berlin palace; and next into the grand hall, hung with black. Eight artificial black columns had been added to this immense hall. Its only embellishments were garlands of cypress, and here again there was too little light.

In about half-an-hour the King returned to his apartments; and, at half-past eight, Prince Henry, Prince Ferdinand and the Duke of Brunswick came to see the same apartments, where they only remained five minutes.

At a quarter-past nine the King went to Prince Henry. The regiments of guards formed under their windows. The canopy was brought; it was of black velvet, surrounded by cloth of gold, and laced with a crape fringe. On the cloth of gold were black eagles. Twelve posts, covered with velvet, supported the canopy; and over them were twelve silver eagles, each a foot high, which produced a good effect.

After the canopy came the state coach[1]; very large, very low, hung with white satin edged with gold fringe, and drawn by eight horses covered with black velvet.

To the state coach succeeded a chariot, in black velvet, on which was a black crown, drawn by eight cream-coloured horses, in black velvet harness, on which were fixed black eagles, embroidered in gold. The livery servants, chamber lackeys, heydukes, running footmen, huntsmen and pages followed.

The Princesses, ushered by Messieurs Goertz and Bishopswerder, were at church.

---

1 *Corbillard.* Perhaps the word is here used to signify a hearse.

At ten o'clock the procession began. The place of assembly was the grand hall with the eight columns. A gentle descent had been made from the grand canopy to the door, to which the state coach was drawn up to receive the coffin. The road from the palace to the church was planked, and covered with black cloth. The procession was truly superb, and conducted with great order. The troops formed two lines.

The church was illuminated with wax candles and small lamps; and the coffin was deposited under a cupola, supported by six pillars of white marble. The organ began to play and the funeral service was performed, which continued half-an-hour. The return was not disorderly, but it was not made in procession.

When the guests came back to the palace, the tables were ready spread, and the courses were served up at noon. The guests rose from table at half-past one. The King, Prince Henry, the Duke of Brunswick, and the Princesses, went to Sans-Souci. Such was the manner in which the morning was spent.

There was no comparison to be drawn between this and the funerals of the church of Notre Dame with respect to magnificence, taste, or splendour; but they did everything that could be done, the country and the time considered.

There was much order from the commencement to the close. The music was indifferent, had no effect, no energy, no charm, and was ill-executed: not one good voice, Concialini excepted, who did not sing well.

The tables were well supplied, the viands abundant and select, the servants numerous and orderly. Each of the aides-de-camp general did the honours of a table. French, Rhenish and Hungarian wines were served in profusion.

The King, going to table, led Prince Henry. On every occasion His Majesty saluted with dignity. His countenance was neither serious nor too cheerful.

He testified his satisfaction to Reck, who replied Captain Gonthard had regulated the whole; and that he had no other merit except that of having procured him everything of which he stood in need.

The King wore the grand uniform of the

guards. The Princes were booted. Prince Goethen had mourning spurs, which was remarked.

The King went and returned in company only with the Duke of Brunswick.

LETTER XXIV

September 12*th*, 1786.

THE King departs to-morrow. The order of his journey has undergone no change. He will be back on the twenty-eighth, and again set out on the second for Silesia. I shall probably have a good opportunity, on his return, to speak of finance and of substitutes. Previous to this, Panchaud must absolutely unite with me to form a good plan of speculating in our funds—good for the finances, and in particular good for the King, who is to be allured. Remember the importance of this Monarch.

Bishopswerder increases in credit, which he carefully conceals. Welner, a subaltern creature, endowed with understanding, management, and knowledge of interior affairs; a mystic, when mysticism was necessary to please, and cured of his visions, since the King has required these should be kept secret; active, industrious, and, what is more, sufficiently obscure to be employed without creating jealousy; Welner, I say, appears to gain prodigious influence. He has the qualities necessary to succeed, and even to outwit all his competitors.[1]

I again repeat, Boden ought not to be neglected, by the way of insinuation. He is vain, and should be capable of corruption: for, always suspected of the most insatiable avarice and the basest means, he has lost a place of eight thousand German crowns by the death of the Landgrave of Hesse-Cassel; and, it is said, is driven to expedients. He corresponds with the King, and rather intimately; that which he should often repeat must produce an effect. He is the hero to slay Hertzberg, who, I may add, has not been successful concerning Holland; and in despite of whom Thulemeyer may still be recalled.

Prince Henry still feeds on hopes. I have no doubt that he is cajoled by the Duke of Brunswick. But he is exactly at the same point, except that Hertzberg is not so powerful. The King intends Alvensleben for the French Embassy; a man of high birth, sense and wisdom, as it is affirmed.

---

[1] He is at present absolutely the principal minister.

He is at Dresden. I shall endeavour to study him and shall take him letters.

No person is satisfied; civil and military, courtiers and ministers, all pout. I imagine they expected it would rain gold. I have nothing to add to my prognostics, which may be reduced to this alternative—The nation sacrificed, while affairs continue tranquil, that we may persuade ourselves we govern—The Duke of Brunswick, should perils intervene, and the storm begin to blow.

In the name of business and of friendship, do not forget a plan of operations for finance. Schulemburg is supported, and I have reasons to believe he will not be dismissed. Should I acquire influence in the finance, I would not be his enemy. He will be more serviceable than any other, Baron Knyphausen only excepted, who will never be anything while Hertzberg is in power.

Remember that you have an incapable envoy in Bavaria; and that this will become an embassy of importance at the death of the Elector. If it be meant to place me, which must be meant if I am to serve, had not I best make my first appearance here?

LETTER XXV

Dresden, September 16th, 1786.

I SHALL say nothing particular to you yet of this country, as you may suppose; for who can run and read? Beside, I find the inconvenience of having no credentials, and consequently have not been able to speak with propriety on affairs, except in very general and metaphorical terms.

Stuterheim, the minister for foreign affairs, with whom I have dined, is said to be a very well, a labyrinth of secrecy; and it follows that his subalterns are exceedingly reserved. The ministers here rather give in their *reports* than act. Give in their *reports*, is the consecrated phrase. But I have been so well convinced, by what I have seen under Frederick II., that the King, who governs most himself, is so little the master, and is so infinitely deceived, that I am perfectly aware of the degree of credit which these Court *dicta* deserve.

I have seen Alvensleben. Should he go to France, I do not think he will live long; he is worn out, and only keeps himself alive by extreme abstinence, and an almost total sequestration from society. He is well acquainted with Germany, is said to act with prudence and propriety, is successful in what he undertakes, and has a good moral character. He is not, however, without art, and perhaps he wishes to be cunning. He is not precisely the man for France; but he is a specimen of the fruit of the country; and, for any other use, is some of the best it produces. I imagine you will find him agreeable.

I shall endeavour to get into the currency of the country; but I repeat, while I shall have no credentials, and am left so much in ignorance concerning home affairs, I shall be much more proper to collect literary and written opinions than for any other business; and the thoughts of men are not written in their faces. Nor do you, for example, find in any book that a prime minister has confided his eldest son, on his travels, to such a blockhead as G———; or to a Chevalier du Vivier, who never utters a word that he does not utter an absurdity, and perhaps some that are dangerous. But why has he related that he waited at Hamburg five weeks for permission to take the Viscount de Vergennes to Berlin, on occasion of the accession of the King, and that this was refused? Is he afraid that they should be insensible at Berlin of the affectation of having avoided that Court? I should never finish were I to cite all the incoherencies he utters, the least of which is ridiculous in the extreme. . . .

In reality, if I am to commence as a subaltern in the diplomatic corps, I have no objection to Hamburg; where, exclusive of the great intercourse of the commerce of the North, with which we are unacquainted, and of which we do not sufficiently participate, since we wish to have an envoy there, we ought to have an active person, instead of one from whom nothing is so desirable as that he should be deaf and dumb.

The vast connections there are between the grand emporiums of trade are such, that these posts are never things of indifference. Why do not they bestow a sinecure on M. du Vivier?

LETTER XXVI

Dresden, September 19th, 1786.

There are few *men* here, yet is the machine tolerably well regulated: nothing can better prove that order and constancy are more necessary for good government than great talents.

The extreme credit of Marcolini is to be regarded as a popular rumour. He is a favourite without ascendency (as without merit) at least in the Cabinet; his influence does not extend beyond the Court. At present he is in Italy, and the routine of affairs is the same. Probably some favours which pass through his hands, and which the excessive devotion of the Elector rather bestows on Catholics than on Lutherans, are the real cause of these murmurs; which, however, are sufficiently believed to occasion the Emperor to make a stupid blunder. He has sent here one of the silliest of ambassadors; one O'Kelly, an Irishman; because that Marcolini had married his niece. He thought by this means to have governed everything; but the trap was so palpably gross that no one has taken the trouble to remove the bait.

The ministers who have real influence are Stuterheim and Gudschmidt. The first is very infirm, but prudent, sage, and with understanding enough to know on what subjects he is ignorant, to ask information, and to consult others. He, however, draws near his end. The second does not shew himself to the world. He is affirmed to be a man of the greatest merit; that he has infinite knowledge; that not a single pamphlet, in any language throughout Europe, escapes him; that his judgment is sound, his understanding perspicuous and penetrating, and his temper communicative; which last quality is in him the more compatible with discretion, because he possesses its piety, without its superstitions. He ranks first in the confidence of the Elector; but it must be added he is sixty years of age, and has ill-health.

Among the ministers, we must also enumerate M. Worm, a well-informed man, who possesses some principles of political economy, with information not very common on the general relations of commerce; together with industry, activity, and great quickness of apprehension; but, as it is said, rarely with much justness of understanding. His moral character is suspected. He is accused of not keeping his hands pure from bribery; but it is not the less true that he is of great service to internal government. He appeared to me to be artful, communicative, ironical, subtle, satirical and crafty; but very proper for business in all countries.[1]

Of all the foreign ambassadors, I believe M. Saftzing, from Sweden, to be the only one above, or rather not below, mediocrity. I except the English envoy, who has the character of being an able man, but whom I have not yet any proper opportunity of examining. He is open and complaisant, even to affectation, considering that his character is English. If we except Alvensleben, not one of the remainder deserves the honour of being mentioned.

The Elector is a man distinct from Princes in general, yet he appears to partake of the character

---

[1] No wonder governments, and consequently nations, are vicious, when such are supposed, even by men of considerable abilities, to be the proper qualities for governors.

of the King of England. The consistency of his mind, which is entire, has a small alloy of obstinacy. I spoke but little to him, because of the confusion of the dinner. Etiquette is observed at the table of the Elector; consequently I paid every care and attention to seat M. de Vergennes near the Prince. He speaks with intelligence and precision, but his voice is harsh, sharp and shrill. His dress and countenance seemed to indicate devout and wheedling, but acute and implacable, jealousy. The very ill education of the Electress, her noisy mode of speech, and her unreserved freedom, greatly occupy this Prince to his disadvantage; for, beside that such kind of vigilance ever bears somewhat of the stamp of ridicule, his crabbed figure, rendered more disagreeable by a paralytic affection in the eyes, becomes at such moments restless, disturbed and hideous.

Such, and so ungracious, as he is here depicted, he is a Prince who, from many considerations, is worthy esteem and respect. Since the year 1763, his desire to do good, his economy, his indefatigable labours, his innumerable privations, his perseverance, and his industry, have not for a moment relaxed. He has paid all the personal debts of the Electors; and is advanced in the liquidation of the debts of the state. He pursues his plans with inflexible punctuality. Slow, but not irresolute; difficult in accomplishing, but intelligent; with few resources at a first view, but possessed of aptitude, and the gift of meditation, his only weakness arises from his religion, which yet does not occasion him to exaggerate his rights, or to neglect his duties. One step further and he would have been a bigot, and one step backward and he would no longer be a devotee. It is much to be doubted whether his confessor, Hertz, has the least influence, except in the distribution of some footmen's places. The Elector supports his ministers with uncommon firmness, against all, and to all. In a word, but for him the country had been undone; and, should he have the good fortune to see a duration of peace, he will render it very flourishing. Population visibly increases; the annual surplus of births over deaths amounts to twenty thousand; and the number of the people is less than two millions. Trade, which might be better, is not bad. The army imitates that of Prussia, over which it has the advantage of being purely national; but, to say the truth, Saxony is the least military of all the provinces of Germany. Credit is good, and even great. The paper currency is at par, or nearly; and the interest of money at four per cent. The Cabinet of Dresden is the only one in Europe which has adopted the true principles of coinage. Agriculture is in a state of passable respectability. Manufactures are free; the rights of the people are uninfringed; justice is impartially administered; in a word, all things considered, it is the most happy country in Germany. Yet this is a remarkable circumstance, and excites admiration when we recollect the terrible scourges[1] which have successively, and sometimes collectively, laid this fine, but ill-situated country, desolate.

---

[1] The principal scourges to which the Author alludes, by the epithet of ill-situated, is war; by which its sufferings have indeed been dreadful. Charles V., the Thirty Years' War, Charles XII., and still more flagrantly, the late Frederick, have been its tormentors. That it should recover, as it continually has recovered, from such periodical, such renovating destruction, is a fact remarkable in history, worthy the attention of the philosopher and the highest eulogium on the country.

They are persuaded here that we instigate the Turk; that there is a coolness between the two imperial Courts; and that Russia is in want of men, money and horses. It must be frankly owned that her bank operations have a gloomy appearance. It is supposed we shall endeavour, should it be absolutely necessary, to effect a diversion in Germany, without interfering, except by coming to the aid of those who should be too much exposed to danger. For no one imagines we shall suffer Germany to devolve on one single head, nor even to be divided between two. And, with respect to Turkey in Europe, it is thought that our interest, conjointly with that of England, will, by one means or other, avert the destruction with which it is menaced.

On enquiry, I find the Elector of Bavaria has not properly had an attack. He has only changed his mistress; and when he does so, he alters his regimen to excite venery. It happens on these occasions that he has nervous affections, which resemble false attacks, and which will some day bring on a paralytic stroke. His life is not depended upon.

The hostilities of the Stadtholder have produced an effect here greatly to his disadvantage. For my part, I do not think his affairs in so disastrous a state as they seem to be believed. Should we embroil province with province, we shall lose our advantages; it will in vain be urged that the Stadtholder is master of Guelderland; the nobility is numerous in that province, and they form *a public* opinion.

I send you the state of the military in the electorate of Saxony, which is no secret; but I shall also add, by the next courier, that of the public stores, which I procured by a singular accident, the particulars of which it would be useless here to relate. I shall only remark that the custom which the Elector has for several years adopted in his offices, of employing supernumeraries without salaries, might give place to discovery, however well secrets may here be kept.

I shall commit to M. de Vibraye, who is returning to Paris, all the minutes of my cyphers, well and duly sealed, and addressed to you.

※   ※   ※   ※

He does not expect to return hither, and has hopes of the Swedish Embassy.

May not the changes which will take place in the corps diplomatique, by the vacancy of M. d'Adhémard, afford an opportunity of giving me something more agreeable and less precarious than a secret commission, which must end, of course, with the life of a minister who is hastening toward the grave? I hope your friendship will not slumber. You must own others might act with less diligence. If you will take the trouble again to read my despatches as they are here sent, not in cyphers but correct, and will at the same time consider all the difficulties of various kinds that I have had to surmount, and the few means which my cloudy situation can afford, you will not be dissatisfied with my correspondence. Since, for example, Zelle has published the history of the King's disease, I have the satisfaction to perceive the information I sent you was exact. True it is that, under the late King, at at the conclusion of so long a reign, a man knew to whom to address himself; whereas at present it is necessary to discover which are the doors at which you must knock. Yet I think I have given a passable picture of men and things. And what could I not effect of this kind, what could I not discover, had I credentials?

*

LETTER XXVII

Dresden, September 21st, 1786.

I HAVE several times mentioned, and particularly in Numbers XI. and XIX., this Boden; I can only refer you to the circumstances you will there find.

As to the person named Dufour, whose real name is Chauvier, and who was a journeyman barber in France, had I thought it of any importance, I should have spoken before, and given his character at full; for he is one of the circuitous paths pointed out to me by Prince Henry. He certainly had influence over the Heir Apparent, which he obtained :—

1. Because he was persecuted by the late King, by whom he had been expelled[1]; so that, in order to return, he was obliged to take the name of Dufour, which is that of a family of the French colonists. And—

---

[1] The Author does not say whether from the Court, or from the country.

2. That he might aid to banish the spleen. He often dined in private with the Prince, who was so familiar with him, some time before his accession, that when wearied with his discourse he would drily bid him hold his tongue.[1] Dufour was one of those with whom I should have made myself intimate, had the King continued to live some time longer; and he was among the persons and things that occasioned me to project a journey to Potsdam. But death suddenly interposed, and I should have sought his intimacy too abruptly; not to mention that subaltern influence has, on the King's accession, totally disappeared.

The person named Chapuis is a man who is not deficient in understanding and address. He was born in French Switzerland. He is the governor of the natural son of the King, and the well-beloved of Madam Rietz. Thinking his acquaintance might be valuable in many respects, I consequently sought it, under the pretence of

---

[1] It is not very clear, from the original, whether it was the Prince who bade Dufour, or Dufour who bade the Prince, hold his tongue. The word *présomtif*, we believe, can only be applied to an Heir Apparent, or we should have reversed the reading.

literature only; but at present Chapuis has not in himself any one point of contact. To run after such people, so circumstanced, would but be to render myself suspicious to no purpose. I mentioned to you, on my return from Rheinsberg (Number XI).—" I have numerous modes of communication, which will develop themselves as time and opportunity shall serve."— But these have been retarded by the accession. Applications of this secret kind can only be made in the depth of winter, and during the Carnival, with utility and safety.

These, generally, are rather *tools* proper for a spy to work with than the engines of influence. Should such people ever have power over foreign politics, the puissance of Prussia must draw to a conclusion. This country must not be estimated by France; there is not here the same margin in which to insert follies, or to correct. And as in general man remains at that point where it is necessary he should be fixed, the King of Prussia will act with circumspection in what relates to foreign affairs.

Not that this should prevent us from recollecting that we ought to guard with extreme caution against a coalition between Prussia and Austria; for this system also is capable of defence. It is even the easiest of execution, and the most splendid; nor would Prince Henry be so averse to it as he himself supposes, should he perceive the least glimmering of hope. Hitherto, indeed, I have not noticed anything that could give suspicion; but I shall more carefully examine whatever might occasion such an event, on my return to Berlin. There can be little danger that I should become languid in the pursuit of this object, having four years ago published my fears of such an event, and having begun to send my static tables of Austria, only that you might attentively consider the immense basis of power which the Emperor possesses, and whose alliance with France I cannot but consider as the masterpiece of Prince Kaunitz, and the type of our indelible levity.

It may be that this power of the Emperor is as much overrated elsewhere as it is the reverse in France; but even this is a reason which may lead to prefer, instead of the perilous honour of being the champion of the Germanic liberties, the easy and deceptive advantage of dividing the spoils. Therefore, delay appears to me more unseasonable than it has been: for it is probable that the King of Prussia, having once pledged himself, will not recede; which seems to be warranted by his personal probity, his hatred of the Emperor, the antipathy that exists between the two nations, and the universal opinion which prevails that the chief of the empire is a perfidious Prince.

Your project concerning Brunswick is certainly excellent, and I shall spare no labour that may tend to give it success. But the man is very circumspect, Hertzberg very vehement, and the crisis equally urgent.

I have conversed with several of the English who are returned from the Emperor's reviews: he behaved there with great affability, and was very talkative. He particularly distinguished a French officer, who had travelled on horseback, that not a single military position might escape him, on his route. The Austrian troops in general manœuvre well, by companies; and even tolerably by regiments; but collectively, their inferiority to the Prussian army is prodigious. Opinions on this point are unanimous. They were not capable of keeping their distances, even when filing off in the presence of the Emperor. This grand pivot, on which tactics turn, is unknown to the Austrians; whereas the Prussians so habitually, so religiously, observe their distances, that any failure of this kind is an error unheard of.

The inferiority of the Austrian army, compared to the Prussian, is attributed:—

1. To the want of a sufficient number of officers and subalterns, compared to the number of soldiers.

2. To the economy, totally anti-military, of the Emperor; who, while the companies nominally consist of two hundred men, does not maintain more than fifty or sixty under arms, and sends the others home, even against their will; so that three-fourths of the soldiers are never disciplined.

3. To the troops being dispersed, kept in petty detachments, and never exercised as a whole; except when they are encamped, where even then they are disciplined by detail.

4. To the very great inferiority of the officers.

The corps of captains forms the soul of the Prussian army, and at the same time is the disgrace of the Austrian, &c.

It is generally affirmed that, should the two nations go to war, there is little doubt concerning which would have the advantage; for that there is no equality between them, even supposing their generals to be equal; and that the contest most certainly would be favourable to the Prussians, during the first campaign. But this equality of generals is not true. Laudon, though still vigorous, cannot wear much longer; beside that, he has often said he never would command an army, unless at the distance of four hundred miles from the Emperor. The abilities of Lacy are suspected, though he enjoys the entire confidence of Joseph II.; and, as it is rumoured, has rendered himself singularly necessary, by the complication of the military machine. No commander in the Austrian army can contend against the Duke of Brunswick, nor even against Kalcreuth, or Moellendorf.

Persons who have come very lately from Russia affirm that the Empress is in good health;

and that *Ermenow* has obliterated her long sorrows for the death of *Lanskoi*. It is also said that Belsborotko gains ground upon Potemkin; but of this I more than doubt.

I have no belief in the facility with which the fifth despatch may be deciphered; I think that in general the cyphers have rather been conjectured than divined. The way by which they are commonly known is the official communication of writings, which is made from one Court to another, and which the minister has sometimes the ill address to send without his accustomed cypher, on a known day. This is a quicksand of which I am not in danger. It is necessary, however, to have a variety of cyphers, and I entreat you will not neglect any occasion of sending me some that are new and more complete.

LETTER XXVIII

Dresden, September 24th, 1786.

Your letter of the fourth of September, which, by mistake, your secretaries have dated the fourth of August, came to hand very late, and I shall reply without written references and solely from memory, in the annexed sheet, to the principal points. I had, indeed, previously answered them; nor do I believe anything has escaped me that it was in my power to learn, or that I have any reason to repent of having sacrificed too much to respect and to probabilities, at the time of the death of the King. Had I pursued my plan, I should have been four days sooner than any of the diplomatic couriers; but I request you will answer me whether it was possible to divine the conduct of our embassy. I disregarded the minute circumstances of death, as I had done that of the news itself: nor could I divine that these, being no longer secret, and having become so easy to examine and describe, should yet have remained secrets to you. I suspected it the less because that certain ambassadors (indeed, most of them) appeared to me so embarrassed, by the completing of their despatches, that I should not have imagined they would have disdained a supply, which was to be obtained with so much facility. Satisfied also with having informed you, thanks to lucky circumstances, of the progress of the disease, in such a manner as few ministers were informed, I despised those particulars that were become public. But there were some that were sufficiently interesting, relative to the two last days of the King, from which a banquet might be prepared at an easy expense; and the poignancy of which not death itself could destroy; relating as they did to a mortal so extraordinary, both in body and mind.

His disease, which would have killed ten men, was of eleven months' continuance, without interruption, and almost without relaxation, after his first fit of an asphyxic apoplexy, from which he was recovered by emetics, and after which the first word he uttered, with an imperious gesture, was SILENCE. Nature made four different efforts to save this her rare composition; twice by diarrhœas, and twice again by cuticular eruptions. Hence it might be said, by the worshippers of a God, that this His image was broken by the Creator himself; and that nature did not abandon one of the most beauteous of her works, till the total destruction of the organs, exhausted by age, had been effected; nor till after a continual warfare between body and mind[1] during forty-six years; till after fatigues and agitations of every kind which signalised this fairy reign, and after the most ruinous disease.

This man died on the seventeenth of August, at twenty minutes past two in the morning; and on the fifteenth, when, contrary to his constant custom, he slept till eleven o'clock, he transacted his Cabinet business, though his feebleness was excessive, without any want of attention; and even with a conciseness scarcely perhaps to be found in any other prince in good health. Thus when, on the sixteenth, the reigning Monarch sent orders to Zelle

---

[1] The French reads—"Contention continuelle *d'âme* et *d'esprit*"; or of *soul* and *mind*: the translator has the misfortune not to understand the distinction.

to repair instantaneously to Potsdam, because the King had remained insensible almost since the noon of the day before, and because he was in a lethargic sleep, the physician, arriving at three o'clock, and finding Frederick II. with animation in his eyes, sensibility in his organs, and so much recollection, not being called, durst not make his appearance. Zelle judged he was past recovery less from the cadaverous odour which exhaled from his wound than because he, for the first time during the whole course of his reign, did not recollect that he had not expedited the affairs of the Cabinet. The conclusion was sagely-drawn; dying only could he forget his duty. . . . Two-thirds of Berlin at present are violently declaiming, in order to prove that Frederick II. was a man of common, and almost of mean capacity. Ah! could his large eyes, which obedient to his wishes seduced or terrified the human heart, could they but for a moment open, where would these idiot parasites find courage sufficient to expire with shame?

LETTER XXIX

Dresden, September 26th, 1786.

CONVERSING with a well-informed man who is returned from Russia, I learnt a fact totally strange to me, though no doubt known to the Count de Vergennes; but, whether or no, one which appeared to me proper to make you acquainted with; and more especially because the project is pursued with greater ardour than ever.

When Hyder Ali, having advanced beyond the Orixa, was at the height of his prosperous success, the inhabitants of the North of Bengal, interrupted in their customary commerce by the conflict between the English and their enemies, brought their iron as far as the frontiers of Siberia, there to find a market. This extraordinary fact was the cause of a remarkable attempt made by Russia, in 1783. She sent a fleet to Astracan, to seize on Astrabat, there to form an establishment, on the northern coast of the Caspian Sea, and thence to penetrate into the interior parts of India. The enterprise failed; but is so far from being abandoned that, at this very moment, a plan may be seen in relief at Petersburg, of the works by which it is intended to fortify Astrabat.

Of all the gigantic projects of Russia this is, perhaps, the least unreasonable; since it is pointed out by the nature of things, and since there is already an inland navigation completely carried on from Astracan, on the Volga, the Mita, the Lake Jemen, the Wologda, the Canal of Ladoga, and the Neva, to Petersburg. Should this plan ever be pursued with activity and success, it must either happen that England will seriously think of an alliance with us, against the system of the North, or she must suffer every sort of advantage to be obtained over her at Petersburg: for the interest of the Russians must then become totally opposite to those of the English; and hence may arise dreadful hurricanes, that may sweep away their puissance in the East.

How many revolutions, how much strife between men and things, shall be occasioned by the development of the destiny of that empire, which successively overawes and enslaves all surrounding nations? It must, indeed, be owned that her influence in each place ought to decrease in an inverse proportion to the multiplicity of these places. But how great is the influence of these augmenting points of contact, relative to Europe! And, without prematurely divining the fate of Turkey in Europe, with an intent to overcharge the picture, should Russia seize on the Polish Ukraine, as the manner in which she is arming on the Black Sea, and disposing of her commerce, seem to indicate and to threaten, how much greater shall they still be? What species of understanding must the Emperor possess, if it be impossible to make him perceive that the Turks and the Poles are less dangerous neighbours than those strange people; who are susceptible of all, capable of all, who become the best soldiers in the world, and who, of all the men that inhabit the globe, are the most malleable?

The various ideas I have acquired here, where I have made a tolerable harvest, will be comprised in a particular memorial. They are not immediately necessary, and are too numerous to be inserted in my despatches. But there was one temptation, which was rather expensive, that I could not resist. The Elector has employed his engineers in the topography of Saxony. Twenty-four maps have already been laid down: they are kept in great secrecy, and yet, by paying some louis for each map, I can have them copied. True it is I recollected that, since I *could*, M. de Vibraye perhaps *has*—but, as we rarely do all we may, or even all we ought to do, it is exceedingly possible this should not be so; and then I should have lost an opportunity that never more could be recovered. This reflection determined me, in the hope that the intent of the act would be its apology; and, as I have not put government to the least fruitless expense, or which did not appertain to the better execution of the office I have undertaken, my surplus accounts, I suppose, will be passed.

*

The Elector of Bavaria is not ill. His new mistress seems only to have been the whim of a day, and his favour again reverts to his former, Madam von Torring Seefeld, originally Minuzzi.

LETTER XXX

Dresden,[1] *September 30th,* 1786.

You have been informed, no doubt, by the courier of Tuesday, of what happened on Monday, at the first Court held by the Queen; but, as I think it is proper I should add some reflections on this subject, I shall begin by relating what passed.

The Princess Frederica of Prussia, who imagined that, according to the very sensible custom of the country, the Queen would sit down to play with natives, and not with foreign ambassadors, had placed the Count d'Esterno at her table; for it was she who arranged the parties. She asked the Queen whom she appointed for her own table. The Queen named Prince Reuss, the Austrian Ambassador, and the Prince of Goethe; but, this species of infantine elephant having, after some consideration, declared that he did not know any one game, the Queen substituted Romanzow, the

---

[1] The scene of this and the two following letters, though dated at Dresden, is Berlin.

Russian Ambassador. The Princess Frederica was exceedingly surprised, but either dared not, or would not make any remonstrances; and, the Queen's party sitting down to play, the Count d'Esterno, with great positiveness, energy, and emphasis, refused to sit down at the table of the Princess; declaring he certainly would not play. He immediately withdrew.

Everybody blames the Queen and the Count. The first for having committed an unexampled blunder, and the second, say the people of Berlin, ought not to have refused the daughter of the King. Perhaps this judgment is severe; though I own I should not myself have refused; because, in my opinion, we should not shew we are insulted, except when we wish to be supposed insulted. And, as I think, it would have been very thoughtless to have taken serious notice of the absurd mistake of a Princess who is the most awkward of all the Princesses in Europe. Neither had Count d'Esterno, rigorously speaking, any greater cause of complaint than any other of the royal ambassadors, among whom there is no claim of precedency. Perhaps, too, it would be imprudent to endeavour to establish any such claim; for this would be very certainly to call that in question which tradition and universal tolerance have granted to us. And here let me observe that, as soon as Lord Dalrymple knew Count d'Esterno had been to complain to Count Finckenstein, he declared he made no demand of precedency whatever; but neither would he suffer precedency from anyone. I should, therefore, have accepted the party of the Princess; but should have said aloud, and pointing to the table of the Queen—" I see we are all here without distinction of persons; and certainly fortune could not have been more favourable to me." (The Princess may really be called handsome.) Had I thought I still owed more to my sovereign, I should, on the next Court-day, have refused the nomination of the Queen; though it must have been a violent and hazardous step, and reparation must have become a public topic; instead of which it is the insult only that is talked of, and that considerably, in the world.

Will the Count d'Esterno, or will he not, at present, accept the first invitation he shall receive?

Should he comply, it will remain on record that, having resented the procedure, he has acknowledged himself second. Yet how may he refuse? I have proposed to Prince Henry, who is the *mezzo termine*, that there should be a Court held by the Queen Dowager, who, from her circumspection and native dignity, is more respected than the reigning Queen; and that Count d'Esterno should be of her party, with the Emperor's Ambassador; which distinction would be the more marked because that this Queen never yet played with foreign ministers. If her mourning for her husband does not counteract this project, it seems to me the best under the present circumstances. The Queen has written a letter to Count Finckenstein, which must have been read to Count d'Esterno, in which is inserted the word *excuse*, and wherein she requires the King should not be informed of the affair. But it is answered the offence was public, and excuses are wished to be kept secret, since silence is required.

The most important and incontestably certain fact is, that there was no premeditation in the matter; that it was the silly giddiness of the

Queen in which it originated; that Count Finckenstein and the whole Court are vexed at the affair; that should the King hear of it he will be very much offended with the Queen, whom he has not seen for these six weeks, and whom he thwarts on all occasions: that he has reversed all the arrangements which in the rapture of accession she had made with the Master of the Household; and that, in fine, never had Queen of Prussia, that is to say, the most insignificant of Queens, less influence.

If, therefore, it be true, on the one part, that the place of every man in this world is that which he himself shall assign to himself, that our rank, already much on the decline in the public opinion, has no need to sink lower; and that Russian insolence, which takes indefatigable strides, has need of being watched and traversed; it is perfectly certain on the other, also, that the proceeding of Monday was distinct and unmeaning, which ought not to be regarded with a lowering brow, under circumstances which may lead from lowering to cold distance, and from the latter to great changes; or, at least, to decisively false steps, to which the Courts of Vienna and London are desirous of giving birth, and by which they will not fail to profit.

Such is my advice, since I have had the honour to have this advice asked. Permit me to add, that Berlin is not any longer an indifferent embassy, but that it is necessary there to be active, yet cautious; amiable, yet dignified; firm, yet pliant; faithful, yet subtle; in a word, to unite qualities which do not often meet. M. de Vibraye means to ask this embassy, should Count d'Esterno retire, or be sent elsewhere. I speak uninterestedly, since I have no reason to presume that, should it be determined to send me on any embassy, I should begin by one of so much consequence; but it is my duty to say that M. de Vibraye, and particularly his lady, are not the proper persons. His understanding is heavy and confined; rather turbulent than active; and timid than prudent. He is more the giver of dinners than the representative of monarchy; he has neither manners, elocution, nor eyes. Madam de Vibraye, who does not want understanding, would be too gay even for Paris; and, to speak plainly, she has little propriety, and less decency. But as she is enterprising, she makes pretensions to dignity with all the behaviour of thoughtlessness; and, as she moulds her husband as she pleases, by suffering him to believe he is absolute master, she renders him morose, uncivil, and rude. Beside which, she sequesters him from the world: and such sequestration must everywhere, and particularly at Berlin, be totally disadvantageous to an ambassador of France. This is one of the errors of Count d'Esterno.

The following is the chief intelligence I hear concerning the King and his administration, relative either to his absence or his return. He is exceedingly dissatisfied with the Stadtholder. It is affirmed you ought to accept the declaration of Count Goertz. I repeat incessantly, that this is the very time when our intentions ought no longer to be suspected; since assuredly, if we wish the destruction of the Stadtholdership, the Prince of Orange has given us a fine opportunity. Prince Henry affirms that, provided he was restored to the right of maintaining order, and not of giving order, at the Hague, and was in possession of a little money, the King would be contented.

I believe he, the King, feels the necessity of not making a false step at the beginning of his political career. One fact, I can assure you, is certain, which is that it was the advice of Hertzberg to march ten thousand men into Holland; and that there was on this occasion a very warm contention between him and General Moellendorf, in the King's presence. By this you may judge of what is to be expected from the violence of such a minister. Still, however, this has not prevented him from being created a Count in Prussia; and, if I am not mistaken, his influence continues.

With respect to domestic affairs, whatever Prince Henry may say to the contrary, the credit of Schulemburg is on the decline: were it only that he no longer appears in the transaction of public business. It is, however, affirmed that he, with many others, is soon to be made a Count, for they are not economists of their titles. The commission for the regulation of the customs begins to strike bold strokes; but they alight on individuals, and are not aimed at general reformation. Launay has received information that the King henceforth can only give him six thousand crowns per annum, in lieu of twenty thousand, the sum he before had; and that he must accept this or resign. Launay, enraged, and the more so because that he has long since demanded his dismissal, loudly declares he will print an estimate,[1] which will prove not only that, in justification of each of his acts, he has a letter from the late King, the fiscal temper of whom he has moderated much oftener than he has provoked, but that he likewise has refused twenty bargains, offered him by Frederick II., which would have acquired him tons of gold. The scandal of this estimate, should he dare to publish it, will be very great; and the analysing of it will rather be a commission of enquiry into the conduct of the late King than of the present state of the customs, which might easily have been foreseen were thus regulated. The commissioners have dismissed Roux, the only able man among the collectors, with a pension of five hundred crowns; and Groddard, a person of insignificance, with a like sum. They have bestowed their places on Koepke and Beyer, with a salary of three thou-

---

[1] *Compte rendu.*

sand crowns, neither of whom know anything; with this difference, that the last is exact, assiduous, and laborious; but both of them are without information, and devoid of principles. Generally speaking, the commissioners themselves have none; nor have they the least knowledge of how they ought to act. Commissions here will all be the same; for, exclusive of the inconveniences that are annexed to them in every country, there is in this the additional one that men of knowledge are very scarce, and they must, therefore, long continue ill-sorted. But the King wishes to satisfy some, bestow places on those who have protectors, and particularly not to have any prime minister. There must be an embargo on business while it remains in this state; and I have many reasons for supposing that no person will, for some months to come, have found his true place, or that which he is destined to keep; we must not, therefore, be in haste to judge.

But we may affirm that the King has exceedingly displeased the people: less in refusing to partake of the festival prepared for his return than in avoiding the street where the citizens had assembled to see him pass.—"He treats us as his uncle did, on his return from the Seven Years' War," say the mob; "but, before imitating him in this, he ought to have imitated the great actions of his uncle."—It must be owned good sense is sometimes on the side of the multitude.

With respect to the domestic affairs of the palace, anyone may remark at the first glance that they are totally in disorder. No master, no one to give directions, no funds assigned; footmen and the household officers govern all. Dufour, or Chauvier (I before explained to you that this was one and the same person), like all the other subordinate confidants without any influence whatever, is rather ill than well treated. Colonel Vartensleben, formerly banished into Prussia because of his intimacy with the hereditary Prince, is supposed to increase in favour. But the two men to be observed are—Welner, to whom it is affirmed are communicated all ministerial papers, the reports on all projects, and the revisal of all decisions; and Bishopswerder, who, beside universal suspicion, talks with too much affectation of having no influence over the King, not to betray himself, in a country where people are not artful enough to say they do not possess a thing which they really do not possess in order that it may be supposed they do.

With respect to pleasures, they are improved upon. One very remarkable arrangement is, that a cook has been appointed for the Princess Frederica of Prussia, the King's daughter by his first Queen; thus she is to have a kind of household; which, if I am not mistaken, is nothing more than a mode, and none of the most moral, of procuring frequent and decent interviews with Mademoiselle Voss, who is capitulating; for she has declared that no hopes of success must be entertained as long as Madam Rietz shall continue to be visited. The latter went to meet the King on his return; then, passing through the city with an arrow's speed, she flew to Charlottenburg, whither the King came, and where she lives. She acts the prudent part of taking charge herself of the pleasures of his Majesty; who apparently sets a great price on any new enjoyment, be it of what kind it may.

It is secretly rumoured, though I cannot warrant its truth, that England is prodigal in caresses, and reiterated offers of a treaty of commerce, on the most advantageous terms; and that Russia itself spares no advances. Certain it is that our enemies and their partisans loudly proclaim that we have lately disbanded ten thousand men; which is sufficient proof, say they, that we have no thoughts of holding the two imperial Courts in awe.

I can also certify that the Grand-Duke and the Grand-Duchess, who long had afforded no signs of existence to Prince Henry, have lately written him very charming letters; but these are no impediments to the licentious discourse of Romanzow, who, on the eve of the King's funeral, asked, in a public company, whether there would not be rejoicings on the morrow; and who has bestowed the epithet of *the illumination of the five candles* on the night of the second, on which homage was paid to the new King, and when a general illumination was ordered. Apropos of homage, Prince Henry is permitted to make written oath, and this favour has not a little redoubled his fumes; he still wagers that

Hertzberg will be disgraced. This Hertzberg yesterday read a pompous account to the academy of his journey into Prussia, and he was suffocated with incense by all the candidates. Nothing could be more completely silly.

I shall conclude with a word concerning Saxony. I do not believe the health of the Elector to be good; he withers visibly; and this is promoted by the violent exercise which he takes from system, and in which he perseveres with all his invincible obstinacy. He will leave no sons, and there is no imagining the hypocritic imbecility of his brothers, who are not married; the result of which is that this fine country is dangerously menaced by future contingencies. Marcolini, as I have said, is on his journey through Italy; and it is supposed that one of his commissions is to seek a wife for Prince Anthony. Prince Henry, who fears lest choice should be made of a Tuscan Princess, or some other of the Austrian alliances, has conceived the project of bestowing the hand of the Princess of Condé on him, by which we should secure the Electorate and the Elector. I give this as I received it.

First Postscript. — Let me add that, with respect to the map I determined to have secretly copied, it is the map of the most important part of Saxony; and one which all the foreign ambassadors, without exception, with M. de Vibraye at their head, are convinced the Elector will not permit his brother to see. I have had a windfall much more valuable; that of the land-survey of 1783, made with great exactitude, and containing a circumstantial division of territorial wealth. I shall have it copied in haste, for which I do not imagine I shall be blamed. M. de Vibraye is quitting Dresden, whither he does not wish to return. It is a pleasant post, and a very excellent one from which to observe the Emperor and the King of Prussia.

Boden is on the road hither; he is imagined to be presumptuous enough to solicit the French Embassy. Either he will be disappointed or the Court of Berlin will act improperly. The King still continues in the intention of sending you Alvensleben. I spoke to you of him when at Dresden, where I conversed much with him; he is certainly a man of information and understanding. M. d'Entragues was intimately acquainted with him, and this friendship has continued. It would be very easy to send for M. d'Entragues, who is at Montpellier; whether it were to conduct or to watch his entrance on the scene of action.

Second Postscript. — Prince Henry was sent for by the King this morning, on business, and invited to go and dine at Charlottenburg. This he has acquainted me with, and desired me to come to him at five o'clock. I can add nothing to this enormous length of cyphering, except that I wish to repeat that the intelligence of the ten thousand men proposed by Hertzberg is fact. It has appeared so important to me, when combined with the affairs of Hattem and Elburg, which seemed to give invincible demonstration that Count Hertzberg had long promised, in the secret correspondence of which I have spoken, the aid of the army of the new King. I say this information appeared so important that I thought it my duty to make it known to the Count d'Esterno, by a channel which he cannot suspect is derived from me.

With respect to Court intrigues here, I have proof that Prince Henry tells everything to Prince Ferdinand, who tells everything to his wife, who, lured by the tempting bribes she receives in ready money, betrays Prince Henry. Luckily the excessive stupidity of this Princess deadens her influence, and congeals the good-will which the King wishes to entertain for her.

LETTER XXXI

Dresden, October 3rd, 1786.

I HAVE had very little time for the courier of to-day, having spent all day yesterday, from six o'clock in the morning till night, at, and in the affairs of, the Court. The ceremony of rendering homage was awful, notwithstanding the narrowness of the place in which the states were received. As moral ideas have a great influence, even unperceived by us, on our physical sensations, this tribute of respect, paid by armed despotism to the nation it governs, this species of paternal colloquy between the Monarch and the deputies, here called the states, establishing in some manner a correlative engagement, to which only a little more dignity on the part of the deputies, and at least the appearance of deliberation are wanting to give pleasure to the heart, fill the mind with sublime and affecting reveries. To a Prince capable of reflection, I would only wish this ceremony to be contrasted with the military oath, and the different emotions they excite to be analysed, in order to lead him to examine whether it be true that a monarchy depends wholly upon force, and whether the pyramid ought to rest upon its basis or upon its point.

After the discourse of the minister of justice (Reek) to the states, after the harangue of the first order (the ecclesiastics), conducted by Prince Frederick of Brunswick, provost of the chapter of Brandenburgh, and after the oath of the nobility, the declaration and confirmation of privileges, the enumeration of titles to be bestowed, made by the minister Hertzberg (the minister Schulemburg is one among the number of new Counts), the King advanced, on a projecting balcony, over which a very fine canopy had been raised, to receive the oaths and the homage of the people. The citizens were assembled, by companies, wards, and trades, in the square opposite the palace. The symptoms of tumultuous joy are here, as elsewhere, the effects of sympathy (I had almost said contagious) between a great multitude of men, assembled to behold one elevated superior to them all, whom they called their Monarch and their Master, and on whom, in reality, depends the greatest part of the blessings or the woes that await them.

It must, however, be remarked that the order was much greater all the day, and at night, than could have been hoped in any other large metropolis. It is true that they distribute here neither wine, cervelats,[1] nor money. The largesses are distributed to each quarter, and pass through the hands of the pastor and the magistrate. It is equally true that the passions of this are scarcely so strong as the emotions of other nations.

The King dined upwards of six hundred people. All who were noble were invited. When the proposal was made to me to remain, I replied that, apparently, only the national nobility was meant; and that, had it been intended to admit foreigners to that favour, they no doubt would have had the honour of receiving such an intimation. All the English, and almost all the French, like me, and with me, retired.

The illuminations were not very great. One was remarked where all the small lamps were covered over by crape, so that the light appeared

---

[1] A species of large sausage.

dim, gloomy, and truly funereal. This was the invention of a Jew, and it was in the front of his own house that it took place. It calls to my mind a beautiful passage in the sermon which preceded the ceremony, and which was preached in the Lutheran church. The minister of the prevailing religion long invoked, and with considerable pathos and energy, the blessings of toleration—" That happy and holy harvest, for which the Prussian provinces are indebted to the family by which they are governed."

I send you the best medals that were struck on the occasion. They are your own. Others are to be distributed among the foreign ambassadors, who, no doubt, will send them home. There were some in gold, but I thought them too dear, the workmanship considered. Each general in the service was presented with a large medal, the price of which is forty crowns. Each commander of a regiment received a small one, of the price of six ducats. The large are good, the small very indifferent. I speak of those that were distributed yesterday; and only of the likeness.

October 4th, 1786.

THE day of homage and its preparations have wholly consumed the time, and obstructed all society, since the last courier; for which reason I have at present little to say. Prince Henry was invited, the other day, principally, as I believe, let him say what he will, because M. de Custine the father, dined with the King. However, His Majesty, before dinner, spoke to the Prince concerning Holland, and complained that the discourse of M. de Veyrac, who had informed Goertz he could not interfere, was in exact contradiction to the promises of the Cabinet of Versailles. The subject of Holland puts him out of temper, as it naturally must; and yet, as I have incessantly repeated—" When could we find a better opportunity of acting disinterestedly than at present; now that the Stadtholder, contrary to reason and all propriety, has taken a violent and decisive part, a few days before the arrival of the advice which was intended to be sent him by the King?"

I have had a very impassioned scene, concerning Holland, with Count Hertzberg: patience, firmness, and something of cunning, on my part; violence, passion, and want of reason, on his. It is evident to me that he is pursuing some secret project concerning Holland.

Apropos of M. de Custine; he made the King wait an hour for him at dinner. It is a melancholy circumstance for France that she should continually be, in some measure, represented by certain travellers, when political affairs are in a delicate state. Our Duke de la F——, amidst an assembly of our enemies, said to the Duke of Brunswick—"Apropos; pray has your Highness ever served?"—At Dresden, a ceremonious and circumspect place, where our embassy has given much dissatisfaction, this same pitiable interrogator, having been shewn a collection of precious stones, the most magnificent that exists in Europe, said to the Elector, at high dinner—"Very good! Yes, indeed, very good! Pray how much did the collection cost your Highness?"[1]

---

[1] A good account of this collection of baubles, which existed in all its splendour under Augustus II., Elector of Saxony, and by which and similar expenses, equally wise, a country so flourishing and industrious was overwhelmed in debt, may be seen in "Hanway's Travels," vol. i.,

A certain M. de P——, a week before the death of the King, dining at Potsdam with the Prince of Prussia, hearing the name of M. de H—— mentioned, exclaimed, "Apropos; I forgot that I have a letter from him, which I am to give you."—And this letter he threw to the Prince across the table. He no doubt imagined such familiarity was exceedingly natural—he who, at Prague, taking leave of the Emperor, seized and shook him by the hand, testifying the great satisfaction he had received at having seen his manœuvres, and renewed his acquaintance with him. And, what is better, it is M. de ——— who relates this anecdote here; which there are

---

chap. 95. The porcelain collection, in splendour and folly, equals that of the jewels. The same Augustus purchased forty-eight china vases of the cunning and covetous Frederick William I. of Prussia, the great merit of which was their great bulk, at the price of an entire regiment of dragoons. The late King of Prussia used, in contempt, to call Augustus III. the Porcelain King; and informs us, in the "History of his own Times" that, when acting in conjunction with the Saxons to conquer Moravia for the benefit of this Augustus, having demanded artillery to besiege Brunn, the Elector replied he had no money to purchase artillery; yet he had lately expended 400,000 crowns on a large green diamond!

Englishmen enough would take care should not have been forgotten, had he not with so much precaution treasured it up in his memory. Wherefore permit such people to travel, whom, by means of the places they enjoy, it is easy to detain at home? There is no possibility of exaggerating the evil which such ridiculous pasquinades produce, at a moment when the ill-designing are so numerous, and who wish that the nation should be judged by such specimens.

Suffer me further to remark, of Messieurs de Custine, that, foolish as the father is, physically a fool, a fool unmeasurable and disgusting, equally is the son a man of great hopes, and appears in all companies with universal success. Not any man so young, with whom I am acquainted, unites so much modesty, so much reason, and such decent timidity, to so great a talent for observation; or, to manners so agreeable and mild, so much caution and wise activity. There is no doubt but that the extravagances of the father display these qualities to advantage in the son; but they exist, and on the most solid basis; for, in all probability, he has taken an aversion for, by being a continual spectator of, the follies of his father. He is one of the scions whom, of all the young men I have known, is most proper to be transplanted into the diplomatic nursery.

The King, all yesterday, was cold and taciturn; not an emotion, not a gracious word, not a smile. The minister Reek, who harangued the states in the name of the Sovereign, promised, in his discourse, that no new tax should be imposed, during the present reign; but that, on the contrary, those that existed should be diminished. Was he commanded to make this promise, or did he venture to make it uncommanded? Of this I am ignorant, and it is a matter of doubt.

The day before yesterday, the King had some domestic brawls, and a scene of jealousy, at Charlottenburg, to support from Madam Rietz. The remembrance perhaps remained with him yesterday; whether or no, the discourse of his minister of justice spoke more pleasingly than his countenance, however agreeable it may in reality be. He is to depart on the fourth for Silesia, and does not return till the seventeenth.

A part of the palace is at present furnishing, but in a simple style.

Public notice has been given that those persons who had been promised reversions of fiefs should appear; that their reversions were annulled, and that they were not allowed to solicit till first there should be a vacant fief, and not for the reversion of fiefs.

I have seen a narrative of what passed in Prussia. The person who wrote it has employed very sounding expressions to depict the enthusiasm of the public, and among them the following phrase of the King: "I have found Prussia very ill, but I will cure her."

Count Katzerling, who had suffered great losses during the Seven Years' War, and met with very ill treatment from the late Monarch, after having been very graciously received by him, has accepted a loan of one hundred and fifty thousand crowns, for thirty years, without interest.

It is said the Bishop of Warmia will be here within three weeks. He is a very amiable man, with the levity of a Pole; and was much in the favour of the Prince of Prussia. The King seems to remember this; he has been treated with much greater kindness than any other person in Prussia.

In November, the King is to balance the statements of expense and receipt.

First Postscript.—I forgot to inform you that, for so cloudy a day, Prince Henry was yesterday highly caressed. He dined and supped with His Majesty, and singly attended him to see the illuminations.

Second Postscript.—I return from Court, the ambassadors were mingled promiscuously; but, as the ministers of the two Imperial Courts were together, the King proceeded in rather a singularly retrograde manner. It so happened (because of the number of Englishmen that were to be presented) that Lord Dalrymple was the nearest to the King's door, and preceded the Imperial Ambassadors. The King began with the latter. He then returned to Lord Dalrymple; after which he descended much lower toward Count d'Esterno and spoke no further to him than by thanking, in general, the foreign Ambassadors for their illuminations. Should this neglect of customary forms continue, I think it would be right to let it be understood that it gives displeasure; for the rumour of the hatred of the King for the French is daily strengthened; and rumour sometimes in reality produces the event it proclaims.

LETTER XXXII

Dresden, October 4th, 1786.

IT appears extremely probable that habit will be the conqueror; and that Frederick-William will never be more than what his penetrating uncle had foreboded. No terms are too hyperbolical to express the excessive negligence of his domestic affairs, their disorder, and his waste of time. The valets dread his violence; but they are the first to turn his incapacity to derision. Not a paper in its place; not a word written at the bottom of any of the memorials; not a letter personally opened; no human power could induce him to read forty lines together. It is at once the tumult of vehemence and the torpor of inanity. His natural son, the Count of Brandenburg, is the only one who can rouse him from his lethargy; he loves the boy to adoration. His countenance brightens the moment he appears, and he amuses himself, every morning, a considerable time with this child,[1] and this, even of his pleasures, is the

---

[1] He died last year.

only one in which he is regular; for the remaining hours are wasted in absolutely inexplicable confusion. His ill-humour the other day, for example, which I had supposed was occasioned by the quarrel at Charlottenburg, induced me to enquire into particulars. It was nothing more than a musical dispute. The King would have a chamber concert. He ordered two-and-twenty musicians to be assembled. It was his intention to have performed himself; his violoncello was uncased and tuned. Fourteen musicians only came; and passions, threats, intemperance succeeded. The valets de chambre laid the blame on Kalikan, whose business it was to summon the musicians. Kalikan was thrown into prison. Duport, the famous violoncello player, and consequently the favourite musician, came to the aid of Kalikan, and gave the King the letter which the valets de chambre had intercepted. His choler then became outrageous; everybody fled; but no further effects have followed this subaltern prevarication. Poor King! Poor country![1]

---

[1] The late despot made drummers of M. Mara (the husband of the celebrated singer) and another musician,

I am persuaded of two particulars; the one that His Majesty has conceived the idea and the hope of becoming a great man, by making himself wholly and purely German, and by hectoring French superiority; the other, that he is already in his heart determined to resign business to a principal minister. He has not perhaps yet owned the fact to himself; but at least he is inwardly convinced it must be so. In this case his last resource will be to call in the aid of the Duke of Brunswick, or of *my uncle*.

The first of these plans is the work and the masterpiece of Count Hertzberg. He has said, and justly said: " There is only one mode of acquiring reputation; which is to impart an impulse to your nation, that under your reign a new kind of glory may take date. This impulse you can only give by acting determinately. What can you ever effect as the partisan of France? You

---

whose name we have forgotten, for having the spirit to disobey an arbitrary mandate; and drummers for hours they remained, to their disgrace, as was intended; but to the disgrace of himself, in reality, and of the nation that will suffer such tyrants, petty as the instance was, to exist.

can only be the feeble imitator of Frederick II. As a German you will be an original, personally revered throughout Germany, adored by your people, vaunted by men of letters, respected by Europe, &c., &c." The explication of the enigma is, that Count Hertzberg imagined this to be the shortest road to make himself prime minister.

But the necessities of accident demand, or will soon demand, a different person. Servile as the country is, it is not habituated to ministerial slavery; and Hertzberg, long a subaltern, rather crafty than able, deceitful than cunning, violent than determined, vain than ambitious, old, infirm, and not promising any long duration of life, will not bend the people to this servility. They must have (for as this Welner, who is so much attended to at present, and whose influence near spectators only can discover, may push his pretensions), I repeat, they must have a man whose rank can quell subordinate candidates; and the number of such men is not great. I can discover but two men of this kind: Prince Henry, and the Duke of Brunswick. To the disadvantage of not living in the country, the latter adds that of being necessarily formidable to a feeble and indolent, but vain and jealous, Prince; and who may imagine that Prince Henry will not commit the same injury on his, the Sovereign's, reputation as a Prince who cannot leave his own country, and reside here constantly as prime minister, without being undoubtedly and conspicuously such. For which reason the credit of Prince Henry daily strengthens, in spite of his ill address. However, he has boasted less within some few weeks; and, instead of not returning from Rheinsberg, whither he again goes during the absence of the King, till the middle of December, as was his intention, he will be here on the same day as his nephew.

Yet, exclusive of the personal defects of Prince Henry, and the errors of which he will indubitably be guilty, how shall we reconcile the German system and the Monarch's hatred of the French to the confidence granted this Prince? The symptoms of such hatred, whether systematic or natural, continually increase and correspond. The King, when he dismissed Roux and Groddart, said, "*Voilà donc de ces B—— dont je me suis défait.*"[1]

[1] "I have rid myself of these ——." The epithet must

The real crime of Roux, perhaps, was that he kept a Jewess whom the Prince of Prussia wished to possess, and obstinately refused to listen to any kind of accommodation. A French merchant brought some toys[1] to shew him, to whom he harshly replied, " I have baubles already of this kind to the amount of seven millions." He then turned his back, and did not utter another word, except to bid him not go to the Queen, for if he did, he should not be paid. The action was far from blameable; it is the manner only that I notice. Boden was passably well received, except that the only consolation he found for his fever was—" Go to Berlin, and keep yourself quiet, for you have a companion that will stay by you these three months."— Boden said to him, " I should have had thousands of messages to your Majesty, had I dared to take charge of them."—" You did well to refuse," replied the King ; and in so rough a tone that Boden durst not even give him the letters of Dusaulx and Bitaubé.

---

be left with the reader; there is no danger he should be more indelicate than the original.

[1] *Des gentillesses*, probably jewels.

Launay is treated with severity, and even with tyranny. He was confined to his chamber while his papers were examined, independent of a general prohibition not to leave Berlin. One Délâtre, his personal enemy, has been opposed to him on all occasions, and has been sent for to become an informer against him; a man devoid of faith or honour; suspected of great crimes; a dissipator of the King's money; an unbridled libellist, and as such denounced by our Court to that of Berlin, which officially returned thanks, two years ago, for our behaviour on that subject. I say he was sent for; because, owing as he does, eighty thousand crowns to the King, would he have ventured to come without a passport, or being asked? It is evident that Launay is persecuted as a farmer of the taxes, and as a Frenchman. It is believed that the collectors and farmers-general will all be dismissed[1] at the

---

[1] *Congédier la régie.*—The late King introduced the French into Prussia, to farm and collect the taxes, at the beginning of his reign. It was one of the most odious of the acts of his internal administration; in which, whenever his own revenues were out of the question, he endeavoured to act for the good of the people. *Endeavoured,* but most

festival of the Trinity; the time when those accounts that shall actually be settled are to be examined. This is the grand sacrifice that is to be offered up to the nation. But what is to supply the deficiency in the revenue? For in fine, the farmers, last year, paid six millions eight hundred thousand German crowns; and it is not only impossible to replace this immense sum, but, knowing the country, it is easy to foresee that the German farmers of finance will scarcely collect the half of the amount.

Of what will the convocation of the provincial and finance counsellors, and the deputies of the merchants, be productive? Of complaints, and not one project which will not be distinct, partial, and in contradiction to the general system; or such as the nature of things presents as a system; for in reality not any as yet exists.

I return, and say, all these projects are contrary to the personal hopes of Prince Henry. Will he make all his passions subservient to his ambition? (He is far from possessing that degree of

---

frequently did not; of this, his innumerable monopolies are proofs incontestable.

fortitude.) Or, does he dissemble that he may obtain power? Of this I do not believe him uniformly capable. I rather fear he is once again the dupe of caresses; which, however, it must be confessed, are more substantial and more marked than they ever had been before. I particularly fear he should be in too great haste, and too eager to gather the harvest before it be ripe; neglecting the care of providing seed for futurity.

The King has given the Minister of Justice, Reek, a box of petrified shells, splendidly enriched with diamonds, estimated to be worth twelve thousand crowns; a similar box to the minister Gaudi, and ten thousand crowns; another of the same kind to General Moellendorf; a fine solitaire to the Marquis di Luchesini; and a diamond ring to Philippi, the lieutenant of the police. He has farther broken up three boxes set with diamonds, of which thirty rings have been made; these he has taken with him to distribute in Silesia.

Take good note, that Launay has not had the alternative of accepting a salary of six thousand crowns, or his dismission; he has merely received information, under the form of an order, that his salary was reduced to six thousand crowns.

Count Hertzberg, this day, gave a grand dinner to foreigners, to which the new Spanish Ambassador was invited, but neither Count d'Esterno nor any Frenchman; which affectation was the more remarkable since all the English, Piedmontese, Swedish, and not only foreign ambassadors but complimentary envoys, were there assembled. Count d'Esterno takes a proper revenge; he gives a grand dinner to-morrow, to which Count Hertzberg is invited.

Postscript.—Mr. Ewart, the secretary of the English Embassy, said to me yesterday, in the presence of fifteen people, Count Hertzberg supporting him with voice and gesture, in these precise terms, " The Stadtholder is, by the constitution, the executive power in Holland; or to speak more intelligibly, he is precisely in Holland what the King is in England." — I replied, in the most ironical and dry tone, " It is to be hoped he will not be beheaded by his subjects." — The laughers were not with Mr. Ewart.[1]

---

[1] The laughers were blockheads.

Boden has sent your packets. The extracts from the pleadings of Linguet, which are excellent (I speak of the extracts), have been perfectly successful. I entreat you will not fail to send me the continuation. You cannot find a better means of procuring me customers than by things of this kind.

There is a demur concerning Alvensleben. It is Hertzberg who supports Goltz.

Number LXXVIII. of the Courier of the Lower Rhine is so insolent, relative to the King of France and his ambassador, that I imagine it would be proper to make a formal complaint. This might somewhat curb Hertzberg, who is the accomplice of Manson, and who may do us many other favours of a like nature, should this pass with impunity. You are not aware of the influence these gazettes have in Germany.

LETTER XXXIII

Magdeburg, October 9th, 1786.

LEAVING Berlin, I by chance discovered the person who has remained four days shut up in the apartment of the Prince of Hesse (of Rothembourg), who is no other than that Croisy, formerly St. Huberty, and once the husband of our celebrated St. Huberty,[1] whose marriage was annulled; Counsellor Bonneau[2] of the Prince of Prussia; and relative to his own wife, a bankrupt,

---

1 The first singer at the French opera.

2 Bonneau is a sea term, in the French language, and signifies buoy. But the word was chosen by Voltaire, because it was an apt metaphor, as the name of a Pandar. From him it is here borrowed, and is several times so applied in this work.

> *Donc, pour cacher comme on put cette affaire,*
> *Le Roi choisit le Conseiller Bonneau,*
> *Confident sûr, et très bon Tourangeau.*
> *Il eut l'emploi, qui certes n'est pas mince,*
> *Et qu'à la cour, où tout se peint en beau,*
> *Nous appellons être l'ami du prince,*
> *Mais qu'à la ville, et surtout en province,*
> *Les gens grossiers ont nommé Maquereau.*
> —*La Pucelle. Chant prem.*

a forger, in a word, a knight of industry, of the most despicable order, and concerning whom all foreigners ask, "Is it possible such a man can be an officer in the French service?" I am no longer astonished that the Prince of Hesse should be coldly received by the King. To come expressly to lay the train to the mine of corruption; and to depend upon it as a certainty that the combustibles should catch fire, from a knowledge of the errors of the Sovereign; to found hopes of success on the ill opinion we have of him, and in a manner to proclaim this knowledge, by a rapid journey from Paris to Berlin, destitute of all other pretext; since the Prince of Hesse and his minion have stayed only five days, and are already gone back to Paris; this is at once to display foolish cunning and contemptible conduct. I imagine it is of importance that we should tell the King aloud, and with the strongly marked, ironical tone of disdain, which shall make him feel, without debasing ourselves to speak more openly, that this manœuvre was totally unknown to our Cabinet; for I am persuaded, from some half-phrases which I have heard those who wish us ill drop, that they do not desire anything better than to fix this blot upon us.

I have travelled through Brandenburg to Magdeburg with Count Hatzfeldt, who had been sent by the Elector of Mayence to compliment the King on his accession, and Baron Geilling, sent for the same purpose by the Duke of Deux-Ponts. The latter, formerly a captain of hussars in our service, is a handsome blockhead, who could only have been chosen because he is the brother of Madam Eixbeck, the Duke's mistress. Count Hatzfeldt is a man of great urbanity, and whose knowledge and understanding are deserving of esteem. It seems he will remain some time at Berlin, that he may discover what shall be created out of the chaos. I conversed much on Mayence; the Elector is better, but does not promise any length of life. The two persons who, in all appearance, are most likely to succeed him are Feckenberg and Alberg. The first is wholly Austrian, the latter a man of abilities, of whom the highest opinion is entertained, whose political inclinations are little known, and who dissembles, like Sixtus V. while yet a monk.

That Court at present seems to be exceedingly averse to the Emperor, who every day, indeed, by a multitude of traits, both private and public, and which are really inconceivable, increases universal hatred. It is impossible to depict the effect which his answer to the request of the Hungarians produced—*(Pueri sunt pueri : pueri puerilia tractant)*—together with the violent abolition of all their privileges. But, on the one hand, the great landholders are at Vienna, there enchained by their places, and almost kept under a guard, so that they are in truth the hostages of the slavery of the Hungarians; and, on the other, the aristocracy being excessively odious to the people, there is in this superb and formidable country neither unity of interest, nor centre of concord. The regular troops are, beside, posted, and provided with artillery, supported by veterans, colonists, &c., &c.

An Englishman, very much my friend, and a man of excellent observation, whom I have happened to meet with here, and who has visited all the camps of the Emperor, while speaking in raptures of those formidable pillars of his power, Hungary, Moravia, Bohemia, and Galicia, &c.,

confesses that the inferiority of his troops, compared with the Prussian army, has infinitely surpassed his expectation. He affirms it is impossible, either relative to the individual or collective information of the officers or to the military talents of the Emperor, which are in reality null, insomuch that he appears incapable of conceiving such complicated evolutions—he affirms, I say, it is impossible to compare the two nations: with this difference, that the Emperor, like Cadmus, can make men spring out of the earth; and that the Prussian army, once annihilated, will be incapable of renovation, except from its treasury. Should *a man* once be seated upon the Austrian throne, there will be an end to the liberties of Europe. The health of the Emperor is supposed not to be good; his activity gradually decreases; he still, however, surpasses his real strength, but his projects seem like the wishes of an expiring patient who raves on recovery. He is supposed at present to be on very cool terms with the Empress of Russia.

LETTER XXXIV

Brunswick, October 14th, 1786.

THOUGH I ride post, you perceive it is not in the spirit of dissipation. Alas! what mode of life in reality less corresponds with my natural inclination than that indolent activity, if so I may call it, which hurries me into every tumult, and among the proud and fastidious, to the utter loss of time! For such is the general consequence of the confusion of society among the Germans, who converse as they call it *between themselves* although thirty persons should be present. Thus am I robbed of study, deprived of my favourite pursuits, my own thoughts, and forced incessantly to comply with forms so foreign, not to say odious, to my nature. You yourself, who lead a life so full of hurry, but who, however, associate with the chosen few, in despite of all the gifts of nature, you must feel how difficult it is abruptly to pass from the buzz of men to the meditations of the closet. Yet is this indispensably necessary, in order to manage the *aside* speeches, by which the current news of the day is acquired and consequences divined. We must gallop five days with the Prince, and pursue all the physical and moral meanderings of the man, in public and in private, before we can obtain the right, or the opportunity, to ask him a question; or, which is better, to catch a word, which may be equivalent to both question and answer.

But who knows this better than you? I only wish you to understand my excursions are not the effect of chance, and still less of whim. Let me add that each of my journeys improves my local knowledge, a subject on which I have made it a law not to be easily satisfied. I hope that, among others, you will perceive by my memorial on Saxony, and by that on the Prussian States, which are, in reality, works of labour, and which you will not have a sight of for some months to come, that I have profoundly studied the countries which I wished to understand, and as ardently in men as in books; with this difference, however, that I scarcely dare confide in the mere assertion of the best informed man, unless he brings written proofs.[1]

---

[1] Are there not, *cæteris paribus*, as many written as related lies?

The necessity of that species of superstitious conscientiousness with which I am almost mechanically impressed, whenever I take up the pen, has been demonstrated to my own mind too often for it ever to forsake me.

Yet whither am I travelling in this painful road? If I may depend on the few reports which your friendship has deigned to make me of the sensation which my despatches have produced, when corrected, arranged and embellished by you (for how is it possible for me to correct that which I write at the moment, by snatches, with lightning-like rapidity, and without having time to read?), they have given satisfaction. If I judge by the reiterated symptoms of the extreme inattention which long silence supposes, on questions the most important, on requests the most instantaneous, and sometimes of absolute forgetfulness of the greatest part of these things, I should be induced to believe that my letters are read, at the most, with as much interest as a packet would be, the materials of which are tolerably clear and orderly, and that the reading produces not the least ultimate effect. Should this be so, is it worth the trouble (I put the question to you, whose energetic sentiments and high thoughts so often escape, notwithstanding all the contagion of levity, carelessness, egotism, and inconsistency which exhale out of every door in the country which you inhabit), is it right, I say, that I should sacrifice, to an interest so subordinate as that of curiosity, my inclinations, my talents, my time, and my powers? I believe you know me to be no quack; you know it is not my custom to speak of my pains, and of my labours, in fustian terms. Permit me then, my good and dear friend, to protest that they both are great. I keep three men totally occupied in mechanically copying the materials I have arranged. I am assisted by the labour and the knowledge of several; all my moments, all my thoughts are there, thence depart, and thither return. Should the product be no greater (and I may say to you that you cannot yet estimate the whole product, for the greatest of my labours are still in my desk),[1] it must either be the fault of my own incapacity or of my situation; perhaps

---

[1] The author no doubt refers to his "Histoire de la Monarchie prussienne."

of both, and perhaps also of the latter only. But here I am wholly, and as a man of thirty-seven ought not to be wholly, devoted to nullities; for nullities they are if nothing be produced, nothing effected, either in behalf of myself or others.

If, therefore, anything *be* produced, afford me some proof of it; and when, for example, I ask any question, for the purpose of more effectually executing my trust, let it be answered. When I say it is necessary I should have a plan of operations of such or such a kind to propose, because that I shall be immediately questioned on the subject, and shall lose an opportunity which probably may never be recovered should I be caught unprovided, let such a plan of operations be sent me.

If all this is to have any good effect in my favour, let me be told so; for in my present situation I have great need of encouragement, if it were but to empower me to yield without madness to the impulses of my zeal. I say without madness; for, to speak only of the vilest, but notwithstanding the most palpable of wants, when I perceive that I am very unable to make my accounts balance with my present appointments, ought I not to clog the down-hill wheel? And what have I to hope from these appointments, when I recollect how much they are in arrear; and that a change of ministry may increase my personal debts with the sums which my friends have advanced me, for the service of those who cannot be ignorant I am myself incapable of making such advances? Yet, should I stop, is there not an end to all utility from what I have hitherto effected? Shall I then have anything remaining except regret for time lost, and the deep, the rankling affliction of having attached people to my fortunes for whom I can do nothing, but what must be an ill compensation, and at my own expense, for all which they have done for me?

Pardon these expansions of the heart. To whom may I confide my anxieties, if not to you, my friend, my consolation, my guide, and my support? To whom may I say, what is all this to me, since it does not produce me even money? For that I expend in the business I have undertaken, and not in private gratifications. In truth, I should be susceptible of no other, were the hoped futurity come, and I had no dependents. You well know that money to me is nothing, at least when I have any. Where am I going, whither leading others? Have I made a good bargain by bartering my life, stormy as it was, but so mingled with enjoyments of which it was not in human power to deprive me, for a sterile activity, which snatches me even from the frequent and delightful effusions of your friendship? You are to me but a statesman; you, for the pressure of whose hand I would relinquish all the thrones on earth.—Alas I am much better formed for friendship than for politics.

Post Scriptum, began at Helmstadt, and finished at Brunswick, *October* 14*th*, 1786.

They write from Silberberg, in Silesia, that the King's carriage has been overturned, and that he has received contusions on the head and on the arm. The coachman, it is added, expired on the place. The news reached me yesterday, at Magdeburg, and the same has been written to General Prittwitz; it probably exceeds the truth, but is not wholly without foundation. The extreme agitation of the Duke of Brunswick and my own emotions made me profoundly feel the fortunes that rest on this Monarch's head. The Duke immediately sent off a courier; and, as I shall follow him to Brunswick, where he wishes to speak to me at large concerning Holland, I shall learn more circumstantial intelligence, and such as will be indubitable. I have not time to add a single word; I write while the horses are changed.

From Brunswick, October 14th, 1786.

Not having found an opportunity of sending off these few lines, I continue.

I arrived here two hours before the Duke. As soon as he came to Brunswick, he wrote to me with a pencil, on a slip of paper—

" I spoke yesterday evening, before I departed, with the minister Count Schulemburg, who had left Berlin on the eleventh. He is in absolute ignorance of the alarming intelligence by which we were so much affected; and, as I have heard nothing on the subject since, I begin to have better hopes. I expect my courier will arrive early in the morning. I write you this, *Monsieur le Comte*,[1] from my mother's, and I hope you will do me the favour to come to me early to-morrow morning and dine with us."

It appears to be very probable that no material harm has happened to the Sovereign.

The splendour of the talents and urbanity of the Duke appeared perfect at Magdeburg. Nothing could be more awful than his manœuvres, nothing so instructive as his school, nothing so finished, so connected, so perfect, as his conduct in every respect. He was the subject of admiration to a great number of foreigners, who had crowded to Magdeburg, and he certainly stood in no need of the contrast which the Duke of Weimar and the Prince of Dessau afforded; the latter the weakest of men, the former industriously labouring to be something, but ill provided with requisites, if we are to judge him by appearances. He might and ought to become a Prince of importance. Accord-

---

[1] My Lord would be too strong an expression: there are but few foreign Counts who in wealth and dignity are equal to the idea which the English word Lord conveys; and the epithet Count, when the courtly Duke of Brunswick speaks, would be too familiar.

ing to all probabilities, however, Saxony will devolve on him for want of children in the Electoral branch; and it is an afflicting perspective to contemplate the destruction of all the labours of the worthy Prince who at present governs the country; and who, tormented in his childhood, unhappy in youth, and truly respectable in manhood, will perhaps descend to the tomb with the bitter affliction of feeling that all the good he has done will be rendered ineffectual.

* * *

I have learnt a fact which will afford some pleasure to M. de Segur, if he be still living. A foundry has been built at Hanover, at a great expense, which has cost the King of England near one hundred thousand livres (upwards of four thousand pounds sterling). The Duke of Brunswick, not being satisfied with his own foundry, had two cannon cast at Hanover; and they were so ill cast that they were soon obliged to be laid aside. It is not to be supposed, when we recollect the connexions between the Duke and the King of England, that this was occasioned by any trick in the founders ; the fact therefore is a proof that they are bad workmen.

By the next courier I hope to send you the exact result of the dispositions of Berlin, and the Duke, relative to Holland. He has promised me a precise statement of the propositions which appear to him necessary, and he did not conceal the extreme desire he had that they should be accepted by France. These Dutch disturbances daily present a more threatening aspect for the repose of Europe ; if not at the present moment, at least from future contingencies, and the coolness and distrust to which they will give rise.

LETTER XXXV

Brunswick, October 16th, 1786.

THE two conversations I have had with the Duke have hitherto been but vague respecting Holland, and indeed almost foreign to the subject. His courier, having brought him the news of hopes of an accommodation, and of the retreat of the person who of all those concerned with M. de Veirac was supposed to be the chief firebrand, having in fine brought him details which lead him to imagine that his interference will not be necessary, or not yet wanted in Holland, he passed rapidly over the country to come to one which is of infinitely greater importance to him; I mean to say Prussia. He only discovered himself to be greatly averse to the party of the Stadtholder, and well convinced that the right of presentation ought to remain such as it was in its origin; that the constitution of Gueldres, Prieseland, and Utrecht, evidently was in want of reformation, with respect to the inconceivable regulation of the magistrates, who are revocable *ad nutum;* that, in a word, the Prince, who from absolute monarchical authority, which he in reality possessed, was sunken into absolute discredit, by conduct the most abject, and the folly of having claimed that as a right, in contempt of all law, all decency, and all popular prejudice, which he effectually possessed, was not deserving of the least support. But that, from respect to Prussia, and particularly to retard commotions, it was requisite to restore him the decorum of pageantry; except that watch should be kept over his connections. And here he explained himself on the subject of Harris, and even concerning Prince Louis of Brunswick, nearly in the manner I should have done myself. In conclusion, however, he not only did not inform me of anything on the subject, but he imperceptibly declined that debate which a few days before he had provoked.

I repeat, there is some news arrived of which I am ignorant that has occasioned this change in his proceedings. My information is in general much too confined. Thus for example it is very singular, nor is it less embarrassing, and, to speak plainly, it is tolerably ridiculous, that it should be the Duke who should inform me of the treaty of commerce signed between France and England, not one of the articles of which I am acquainted with, and on which occasion I know not what face to wear. As my usual method is not to conceal myself behind any veil of mystery, which hides the insignificance of certain ambassadors, the part I had to act was not a little difficult. I should learn a thousand times more were I myself better informed. In this, as in everything else, fortune follows the successful.

Returning to Prussia, it was quite a different affair, for of this I know as much as the Duke His confidence was the less limited and the more profuse, because I presently set him at his ease with respect to Prince Henry, whom he neither loves nor esteems. I perceive with inquietude that his opinions and fears are similar to my own. He is dissatisfied with most of the proceedings and public acts of the King, with that crowd of titles, and that mass of nobility, which has been added so prodigally; insomuch that it will be henceforward much more difficult to find a man than a nobleman in the Prussian States; with the promise made to the Prince of Dessau (whose only merit is such an excess of enthusiasm for mysticism and visionaries that, when Lavater came to Bremen, he addressed the most earnest supplications to him to come and pay him a visit, in order that he might adore him), and perhaps with that given to the Duke of Weimar (who to the same inclinations, and more lively passions, adds greater understanding; but who is too much in debt for his military projects to be otherwise regarded than as a money speculation), to restore the one to and admit the other into the Prussian service; by which rank in the army will be violated, and the army discouraged and vitiated; a system very opposite to that of Frederick II., who said of the few grandees who were employed in his time, "In the name of God, my dear Moellendorf, rid me of *these Princes*." The Duke is equally dissatisfied with that fluctuation which occasions essays to be made on twenty systems at once; with the most of the persons chosen; with domestic disorder; with nocturnal rites; and with the anecdotes the augury of which from day to day becomes more inauspiciously characteristic, &c., &c.

In a word, should I transcribe our conversation, I should but send new copies of old dispatches.

"Believe me," said he, "I may, in a certain degree, serve you as a thermometer, for if I perceive there are no hopes of a firm and noble regimen, and that therefore the day of the house of Brandenburg is come, I shall not be the last to sound a retreat.' I never received money from the King of Prussia, and I am well determined never to accept anything from him, though I mean to remain in the service. It has, as you have seen, been a dear service to me. I am independent. I wish to pay a tribute of respect to the memory of the great man who is no more, and am ready to shed my blood, if that might cement his work; but I will not, even by my presence, become the accomplice of its demolition. Our debts never exceed our abilities. I shall provide in the best manner in my power for my country and my children; these I shall leave in great order. I keep up my family connections. We perhaps shall be the last who will be smote by the overthrow of the Germanic body, because of the confraternity which unites us to the Elector of Hanover. I, therefore, shall no further follow the destiny of the Prussian monarchy than as its government shall maintain its wisdom, its dignity, &c., &c."

At present the Duke despairs of nothing; and in this he is right. He supposes that no person has yet found his proper place: I think like him, and I perceive he hopes his turn will come; of this neither can I doubt, unless the annihilation of the Prussian power has been decreed by fate.

He has informed me of the very singular fact that M. de Custine, the father, has demanded to be admitted into the service of the King of Prussia, and has pretended to disclose all the hostile plans of the Emperor, whose alliance, nevertheless, this same M. de Custine loudly affirms will terminate, with France, the day that Prince Kaunitz dies.

The Duke is very far from being relieved of all his fears concerning the projects of the Emperor, whose puissance and advisers he holds in infinite dread. True it is that his inconsistency should render his designs and the execution of them abortive; that the irrationality of his personal conduct should hasten his end; that the Arch-Duke Francis appears to be a cypher; that among the persons who have influence there is not one formidable man, especially in the army; and that Alventzy and Kinsky, the one manufacturer for the infantry, and the other for the cavalry, possess only ambiguous abilities, &c. But men start up at the moment when they are the least expected; accident only is necessary to rank them in their proper place. Condé, Spinola, and the Duke of Brunswick himself, prove that it is possible to be born a general. There is a Prince of Waldeck in the Austrian army, who, it is said, announces grand talents.

The numerous trifling anecdotes which the Duke and I have mutually related to each other, would be too tedious for insertion, and out of their place also here. An anecdote, merely as such, is equally devoid of propriety and information; such will have their turn hereafter; but there is one which relates too much to the Russian system for it to be passed over in silence.

The Czarina has, for some months past, appropriated to herself the possession and the revenues of the posts of Courland, leaving a small part only to the Duke, in order that this branch of administration might not appear to be wholly in the hands of foreigners. Thus does this same Russia, that maintains an envoy at Courland, although there is none at Courland from Petersburg, and that here, as in Poland, proclaims her will to the Duke and to the states, by her ambassador, who is the real sovereign of the country; this Russia, that, for some years past, has unequivocally and openly declared a certain canton of Courland appertained to her, and without seeking any other pretext than that of giving a more uniform line to her limits, makes no secret of not understanding any other code, any other claims, any other manifestoes, than those which the Gauls alleged to the Etruscans—" Our right exists in our arms. Whatever the strong can seize upon that is the right of the strong."—She will one of these days declare Courland is hers, that the Polish Ukraine is hers, and that Finland is hers. And, for example, this latter revolution, which will be a very salutary one to her because that she will then truly become unattackable, and almost inaccessible, to all Europe united, will be effected, whenever she shall make the attempt, if we do not take good heed. Be the day when it will that I shall be informed of this having taken place, and even of the new system of Sweden being totally overthrown, I shall not feel any surprise.

The Duke also told me that the Emperor is greatly improving his artillery; that his six-pounders are equivalent in force to our former eight-pounders; and to this advantage they add that of lightness, in so great a degree, that only four horses are necessary to draw them, while even in Prussia six are still requisite. As well as I remember he attributes this double improvement to the *conical*[1] construction of the chamber. I only relate this that you may verify the truth of the fact, by people who are acquainted with such affairs; the diminution of two horses in eight being a thing of infinite importance, and the more so as there would be a servant the less.

The manner in which I have been received

---

[1] *Faite en poire* (made in in the form of a pear).

by the Duke was infinitely friendly on his part, though somewhat participating, as far as relates to freedom of conversation, of my equivocal mode of existence at Berlin. I believe I may without presumption affirm I am not disagreeable to this Prince, and that, were I accredited by any commission whatever, I should be one of the most proper persons to treat with him with efficacy. This able man appears to me to have but one weakness, which is the prodigious dread of having his reputation injured, even by the most contemptible Zoilus. Yet has he lately exposed himself to vexatious blame in deference to his first minister, M. von Feronce, which I cannot comprehend. This M. von Feronce, and M. von Munchausen, grand master of the Court, a man who is reported to have little delicacy concerning money matters, have farmed the lottery, an action shameful in itself, and which I cannot reconcile to Feronce, who is really a man of merit. Two merchants, named Oeltz and Nothnagel, have gained a *quaterne*, which is equivalent to the sum of eighteen thousand crowns. The payment of this has not only been refused, but as it was necessary to act with fraud to effect their purpose, the merchants have undergone numerous oppressions; they have even been imprisoned; all which acts they have lately published in a printed case, which contains nothing but the facts concerning the suit, and have laid an appeal against the Duke, or against his judges, before the tribunal of Wetzlar; I own I do not understand this absence of firmness, or of circumspection.

October 17th, 1786.

Postscript.—I have just received authentic intelligence concerning the King of Prussia. It was one of his chasseurs to whom a very serious accident happened; the Monarch himself is in good health, and will arrive on the eighteenth or the nineteenth at Berlin.

I learn, at the same time, that Count Finckenstein is dying of an inflammation of the lungs, with which he was seized after a very warm altercation with Count Hertzberg, on the subject of Holland. His life is despaired of, and his loss to us will be very great; as well because he was absolutely ours, as because that, being a temporizer by nature, he would have acted as the moderator of Prince Henry. He would also have directed the conduct of Mademoiselle Voss, after the fall of virtue; and finally because Hertzberg will no longer have any counterpoise. With respect to the latter point, however, I am not averse to suppose that the time when this presumptuous man shall be in absolute discredit may but be the more quickly accelerated. Yet, not to mention the sterility of subjects by which this epocha may be retarded, who shall answer that a man so violent, and wholly imbued as he is with the hatred which the Germans in general bear the French, will not venture to make some very decisive false steps?

The Duke of York arrived here this evening, and had he been the Emperor he could not have been treated with more respect, especially by the Duchess and the courtiers. She indeed is wholly English, as well in her inclinations and her principles as in her manners; insomuch that her almost cynical independence, opposed to the etiquette of the Courts of German Princes, forms the most singular contrast I know. I do not, however, believe that there is any question concerning the marriage of the Princess Caroline, who is a most amiable, lively, playful, witty, and handsome lady; the Duke of York, a puissant hunter, a potent drinker, an indefatigable laugher, destitute of breeding and politeness, and who possesses, at least in appearance, much of the Duke de Lausun, as well in mind as in person, is inspired with a kind of passion for a woman married to a jealous husband, who torments him, and will not suffer him to fix his quarters. I know not whether he will go to Berlin. The versions relative to him are various. Some affirm that, after having been an unbridled libertine, he feels a returning[1] desire of doing his duty. For my own part, I find in him all the stiffness of a German Prince, with a double dose of English insolence, but wanting the free cordiality of that nation.

---

[1] The attention this young Prince at present pays to his public duties, civil and military, and the independent firmness with which his public conduct has so recently been stamped, are the best commentary to this text.

LETTER XXXVI

Brunswick, October 27th, 1786.

I HERE send you the continuation and conclusion of the preceding dispatch, to which I add the translation of a pamphlet, the singularity of which is increased by having appeared at Vienna, with the permission of the Emperor, who, to the communication made by the censor, has added these very words—" Let this pass among others."

This is but a trifle compared to that caprice which three days afterwards induced him to release the unfortunate Szekely, whom the most powerful remonstrances could not save, and whose cause is here[1] ill enough defended. For what conclusions might he not have drawn from the confidence with which he imparted to the Emperor the situation of his accounts, from the disorder by which they had been brought into this state, from the ardent supplications he made him to purchase for the public a well-tried chemical secret at such

---

[1] By the word *here*, the author means in the pamphlet, to which the reader will immediately come.

a price as would have completed the deficiency in his accounts (I say completed, for Szekely and his family had paid the greatest part of the deficiencies), and from the answer of the Emperor himself.—" Do you address yourself to me as to a friend, or as to the Emperor? If to the former, I cannot be the friend of a man who has not been faithful to his trust. If as Emperor, I would advise you to go in person and make your declaration to the courts of justice."

This fact, which I have learnt since my arrival at Berlin, attended with most aggravating circumstances, is one of the most odious I can recollect, yet might I relate fifty of the same species.

※　　※

Free Observations on the Crime and Punishment of Lieutenant-Colonel SZEKELY, *of the Guards, by a Friend of Truth,* 1786.

LET the voice of truth be heard, let her at present be seen without disguise, without veil, in all her awful nakedness. Hear, ye incorrupt[1] judges. I am about to speak of the crime and punishment of Szekely. My heart melts, but my words shall be impartial. Hear and pronounce sentence on me, on Szekely, and on those who pronounced sentence on him.

Szekely announces a deficiency in the regimental chest of the guards, and the disorder of his accounts; and after some pretended exami-

---

[1] From the life of Baron Trenck, from the present fact, and from numerous others, it appears that the appeal and the apostrophe are absurd. Trenck informs us that his judges, after having held their offices for a succession of years, were at last condemned to be the common scavengers of Vienna. The picture he gives of their intrigues, their corruption, and their vices, is beyond conception horrible. How can man dare to vaunt of the wisdom of the age, which has not yet discovered that justice, in its most extensive sense, is the most necessary, as well as the sublimest, attribute of man?

nations is brought before the Council of War. Ninety-seven thousand florins of the empire have disappeared; but Szekely had placed his whole confidence in the Sieur Lakner, who is deceased, and who was the only keeper of the keys of the chest. Szekely had more than once declared that he himself was a very improper person to have pecuniary matters committed to his charge, and that he never had revised nor verified the accounts of the regimental chest confided to his care. He therefore cannot be suspected of personal fraud, especially when his regiment renders justice to the goodness of his manners, and unanimously points out the cashier Lakner as a person who was debased by meannesses, and rendered suspicious by incurring expenses infinitely above his fortune.

This, it is very true, was an exceedingly culpable negligence, but such was the only crime of Szekely; and it was for this reason that the council of war condemned him to be imprisoned six years in a fortress. The punishment was doubtless in itself sufficient, since Szekely, in effect, and according to the language of the civilians was *Nec confessus nec convictus* of any prevarication; yet was it aggravated by the Aulic[1] council of war, which was commanded to make a revision of the process, and which increased his detention to a duration of eight years. Was this tribunal ignorant, then, that it is a custom with our *most gracious* Monarch himself to increase the severity of all sentences pronounced against criminals? Let us, therefore, believe that the judges, on this occasion, were only obedient to the rigour of the laws; but the after decision of the Emperor will most assuredly appear inconceivable. The following is the judgment which this Monarch uttered—yes! uttered, yet did not blush:—

"Szekely must without hesitation be broken, declared incapable of military service, and delivered over to the civil officer, who shall convey him to the place where the crime was committed in Vienna, where he shall stand in the pillory for three successive days, and remain two hours each day on a scaffold, in the high market-place, that

---

[1] We cannot find a better parallel to this *Aulic* council than our formerly infamous Court of Star Chamber.

his example may be of public utility. As a favour, and in consequence of his age, I limit the eight years' imprisonment to which he is condemned to four, during which he shall be confined at Segedin, a penal prison of the civil power of the Hungarian states, where he shall receive the same allowance for food as is granted to other criminals."

The court of justice made remonstrances to the Emperor, in which it proved that the punishment was much too severe, and entirely contrary to law and to equity; but the Emperor continued inflexible, and thus confirmed his sentence:—

"All superintendents of military chests might, like Szekely, plead that they knew not what was become of the money, even though it should have been stolen by themselves. Whenever there is a deficiency in any chest, and especially of a sum so considerable as ninety-seven thousand florins, there is no necessity for the judge to prove that the money has been taken by the accused person, but the accused person must show that it has not been taken by him; and whenever he cannot demonstrate this he himself is the thief. As soon as Szekely shall have been broken, and shall be no longer an officer, the sentence against him shall be put in execution, and a paper shall be fixed round his neck, on which shall be written—AN UNFAITHFUL STEWARD."

Let us take an attentive retrospect of these supreme decisions.

Szekely is punishable for having been exceedingly negligent; he is the same for having bestowed his whole confidence on a dishonest cashier, of whose pompous luxury he could not be ignorant, since it gave offence to the whole corps of the guards. It was easy to conclude that such a man could not live at an expense so great on his paternal income. It is even probable that Szekely himself, perceiving the disorder of his accounts, and the deficiency in his chest, and terrified by the infamy and punishment inflicted on such crimes, sacrificed much to alchemy and the occult sciences, in the hope of making gold, and of thus freeing himself from his embarrassments. This, no doubt, was a folly at which all men of sense would grieve; it is not, however, the less possible. It is certain that the love of chemistry was the ruling passion of Szekely, and that he indulged his inclinations the more because he expected some time thus to recover his losses. To this excuse let us add the extreme ignorance of which he accused himself in all that related to pecuniary affairs.

True it is that, with such a conviction of his own incapacity, he never ought to have taken charge of a regimental chest; but were all those who are in possession of places the duties of which are far beyond their abilities, obliged to abdicate them, what vast deserts would our public offices afford! Rabner encourages three different species of men,[1] by saying, "On whom God bestows an office he also bestows a sufficient degree of understanding for the exercise of that office." Szekely would not indubitably have adopted this opinion, could he have foreseen the evil consequences of his presumption.

Was not that flattering letter which was addressed to him by Maria Theresa, of glorious memory, in which, while she gave the highest praises to his probity and loyalty, this august Sovereign confided to his care, without any pre-

---

[1] I know not why three different species, or what three; I can but follow my author.

caution, the regimental chest of the guards, an authentic testimony in behalf of his honour? Has it been meant by the forgetfulness of this distinction to add a new outrage to all the ingratitudes with which some have sullied themselves, relative to this immortal Empress? Was it intended to tax her with that levity, that silly credulity, which blind confidence produces? Alas! in despite of all the defects which envy so gratuitously imputes to her, Maria Theresa never was surrounded by such an army of knaves as those from whom all the rigour of the present Sovereign cannot preserve us. So true is it that gentleness and love, from a Prince toward his subjects, are more efficacious means, to preserve them within the bounds of duty, than all the violent acts tyranny can commit.

I return to Szekely and affirm it is impossible that this letter from the Empress Queen, though in some sort the pledge of the fidelity of Szekely, can serve as an excuse to the Prince of Esterhazy, whose personal negligence cannot be justified. Did not his right, as chief of the guards, impose it on him as a law to examine the regimental chest of Szekely? And is not such an infraction of the duties of his place most reprehensible?

Still less can be offered in defence of the fault committed by the Hungaro-Transylvanian chancery; since, according to its instructions, it was in like manner bound to inspect the administration of Szekely. But none of the acts of this superior Court ought to inspire astonishment, since it is no longer distinguished, except by disorder and ill faith; since its responsibility is no longer anything but a word; and since its ideas of exact calculation, and of receipt and expense, are exactly as just as those of Brambille[1] are on physic.

Judges, ye have condemned Szekely. Be it so. Act worthy of your office. Punish his super-

---

[1] This Brambille is first surgeon to the Emperor, by whom he has been ennobled, and who has made him inspector of the medical and chirurgical academies. He is said to be an ignorant quack, and a violent satire has lately been written against him, which if report speak truth is very pleasant. This satire has been licensed and publicly sold at Vienna, which is another singular fact, and tends to prove that pasquinades will be much rather suffered, in Austria, than instructive and free works.

intendents also, who have by a non-performance of their duty placed him on the brink of that abyss into which you headlong plunged him, without humanity, and void of shame.

The Kings of Europe have all reserved to themselves the most benevolent of prerogatives; that of pardoning the guilty, or of softening the pains the sentence inflicts by which they are condemned. Joseph alone persists in other principles, more conformable to the feelings of his heart. He aggravates the punishment of the wretched. Alas! this no doubt is but to enjoy the ecstatic pleasure of terrifying his people, by the exercise of the most unlimited despotism. Unfortunate Szekely! ill-starred man! I pity thee. Thou fallest a victim to the splenetic temper of the Monarch! Perhaps, at the very instant when he pronounced thy doom, a troublesome fly stung his brow, and thy dishonour was his vengeance. Deplorable sacrifice of a tyrannical and barbarous heart, yes, I pity thee! Men of worth, men of justice, what must the Monarch be who can *add* to the rigour of the judge?—A tyrant!—What can the Monarch be who tramples under foot the rights of humanity?—A tyrant!!—What can the Monarch be who can make the laws and the justice of his kingdom his sport?—A tyrant!!!—What can the Monarch be who in criminal decisions shall act only according to his caprice?—A Joseph!!!!

A Joseph!—Oh, God! Great God! What then is man? A poor and feeble creature, whom an imperious oppressor may at any moment reduce to dust; or may rend his heart, extort his last sigh, by the seven thousand raging torments which the Hydra with seven thousand heads in sport inflicts.

Dreadful image! Ignominious to humanity, yet wofully true, wofully exact, wofully confirmed by experience!—Does not a Sovereign who increases the rigour of sentences openly proclaim—"Ye judges, whom I have appointed to judge according to law and equity, ye are prevaricators; ye have betrayed your trust, falsified your consciences, and have endeavoured to practise deceit upon me"?—Such magistrates, therefore, ought not to be continued in office; for, to suffer them still to be judges is to approve their conduct, and confirm their judgment. But, destructive as the thunderbolt, the Monarch, addressing them, exclaims—" Your sentence is too mild ! It is my will arbitrarily to increase punishment, that I may prove myself the master of life and death !"— What language, oh, God ! from the mouth of a King whom thou hast appointed to be our protector, and not our tyrant !

Szekely would never have been condemned, had he not been intimately connected with the Freemasons. When the Emperor pronounced sentence against this unfortunate man, he forgot himself so far as to say, " I will let those gentry (the Freemasons) understand there is no efficacy in their protection."

Where then is the equity of a Monarch who thus prostitutes the power he is in possession of, to the destruction of one of the members of a society which he detests ? Who would not smile contemptuously at the poor malice of a peasant who should go in search of his neighbour, after twilight, that he might unseen give him a fillip on the nose, run away, and divert himself with having played him so cunning a trick. Oh,

Justice! Justice! Shalt thou for ever have eyes that thou mayst not see?

Yes, debased, corrupted was the mouth which increased the rigour of the sentence of Szekely, who previously had been destined to languish eight years in prison.—Joseph has diminished the term of his detention. And are these then thy favours, sceptred executioner? Yes, this favour granted to a man of quality, who was for three successive days exposed in the pillory, resembles that which a criminal, condemned to the gallows, should receive from thee, whom thou shouldst permit to be racked upon the wheel, because he was too feeble to mount the ladder.

Couldst thou have survived the shame of such a crime, had not thy people themselves applauded thy fury? The curiosity with which all Vienna enjoyed the spectacle the wretched Szekely afforded, proves that the manners of thy subjects already partake of thine own barbarity. But let them tremble, slaves as they are, bowed beneath the yoke. A new Nero promises new crimes, new horrors!

LETTER XXXVII

Brunswick, October 18th, 1786.

I FEAR there are some waverings in the mind of the King, relative to Holland; for the Duke, after the arrival of his courier, and receiving information of the danger of Count Finckenstein, again spoke to me on the subject, with a degree of inquietude which was far from dissembled. The following were his proper words: " Holland will certainly occasion a war, especially should the death of the Elector of Bavaria intervene; do you act therefore as mediators to smother the rising flames. Come, come, the Stadtholder must have a council, without which he can perform nothing; and how shall this council be selected?"

I replied to the Duke, that I was not sufficiently acquainted with those affairs to give any opinion on the subject, but that I was going to make him a proposition which he must only regard as ideal, and coming from myself, although it might by no means be impracticable :—

" Now that I know how far I can depend upon

your prudence and your principles," continued I, "I am certain that you will see the affairs and the conduct of the Stadtholder in their true light; that you will not imagine friendship in politics can have any other basis than interest; or that we ought to renounce our alliance with Holland, in order that the Princess of Orange may nightly enjoy more agreeable dreams; that you cannot but comprehend how much it is impossible for us to place any confidence in Count Hertzberg, who, relative to us, is frenetic, and how much our distrust may be increased should our sole counterpoise to this violent minister disappear by the death of Count Finckenstein. I shall, therefore, thus far, willingly step forward to say that it appears to me very probable France will be inclined to treat on this affair with you singly, should the King of Prussia consent that you should be solely trusted with the business on his behalf; and, as I may say, should you be made arbitrator. I feel how important it is to you, to us, and to all, that you should not endanger yourself in the opinion of His Majesty. There are already but too many causes of distance existing between you, and the country is entirely lost if the necessities of the times do not oblige you to take the helm. But, should you find the crisis so alarming as to dread decisive events should be the consequence, it appears to me that then it will no longer be proper to keep beating against the wind. For, if the King of Prussia be fated to commit irreparable faults, it would be as well for all parties that he should begin to-morrow, in order that we might the sooner augur what his reign shall be, and choose our sides in consequence. It is for you, therefore, to know in what degree of favour you are with the King. He cannot love you; for never yet did the weak man love the strong. He cannot desire you should be his minister, for never yet did a vain and dark man desire to possess one who was himself illustrious and luminous. But it is neither his friendship nor his inclination that are necessary to you; it is power. You ought to acquire that ascendancy over him which a grand character and a vast genius may ever acquire over a confined understanding and an unstable mind. If you have enough of this ascendancy to inspire him with fears for his situation; to convince him that he is already betrayed to danger; that the sending of Goertz, in your despite (or, rather, without your knowledge, for you were not then at Berlin), is a blunder of magnitude, which has been committed without possessing the least pledge of docility on the part of the Stadtholder; that the inconsiderate letters of Hertzberg form another equal blunder; that this minister pursues his *personal interests*, and those only, at the hazard of depriving his master of *personal respect*, even from the commencement of his reign; since it is very evident that, if he persist in his thoughtless interference (be suppositions as favourable, nay, almost as romantic, as you please), he will only have played the cards of the English, although they have spoilt their own game—if you can make him sensible of all this, you will easily be able to persuade him that he will but be too fortunate in accepting your mediation. And, although mediation is not exactly the phrase which may be employed, because that it does not exactly square with the rule of proportion, such is the esteem in which you are held by the Cabinet of Versailles that, should this negotiation once be committed to your care, all difficulties will vanish of themselves. Such a measure, therefore, would have the double advantage of accommodating the affair, which you regard as the brand of discord, and of teaching the King to feel that he presumes too much if he imagines that, by the sole magic of the abrupt and *tudescan*[1] French of Count Hertzberg, he will be able to preserve the same respect for his Court which a succession of great acts, heroical prosperity, vigilant activity and perseverance, even to a miracle, for forty-six years, have procured it; that he has need of a man whose name abroad and whose influence at home should attract confidence and serve as the key-stone to an arch which, according to its dimensions, has but little solidity; or, to speak without a metaphor, a kingdom ill-situated, ill-constituted, ill-governed, and which possesses no real strength, except in opinion, since its military position is wretched and its resources precarious. For, with respect to the treasury, it will vanish if a hand of iron, yet not a hand of avarice, should not guard it; and, as to an army, who can be

---
[1] German.

more convinced than you are, that years scarcely are sufficient for its formation; but that six months of relaxed discipline may degrade it so that it shall no longer be cognisable?"

This discourse, which fixed the attention of the Duke, and which was particularly intended to divine what he himself imagined he might be able to accomplish, and what he might become, appeared to produce a very great effect. Instead of beginning, as he always does, by ambiguous and dilatory phrases, which may serve any purpose he shall please, he immediately entered into the spirit of my discourse; and after having felt and owned, with an effusion of heart and a penetrating tone, that I presented him a prospect of the greatest honour his imagination could conceive, and which he should prefer to the gaining of six victories, he joined with me in endeavouring to find some means of making the overture to the King.

"I do not imagine," said he, "my situation will authorise the attempt without previous measures. I am more afraid of injuring the cause than of injuring myself; but it is certainly necessary the project should be conveyed to him;

and, should he afford the least opportunity, I will explain everything. Cannot you speak to Count Finckenstein, should he recover?"

"No, for he strictly confines himself to his department. Neither is this anything more than an idea of my own, and of small diplomatic value, since I have no credentials."

"You have but few opportunities of speaking in private to Welner?"

"Very few. Beside, how can that man ever be devoted to you? He determines to act the principal part himself. He is industrious for his own interest, being very sensible that, because of his obscurity, he has an immense advantage over you. Not to mention that he is the intimate friend of your brother, who does not wish your company at Berlin."

In fact, this brother hates the Duke, by whom he is despised, and hopes for favour and influence under the reign of mysticism.

We had proceeded thus far in our discourse when the whole Court, leaving the opera for supper, and the Duke of York, by entering without any precursor, obliged us to break off. He has appointed to meet me this morning, the day of my departure, at nine o'clock, and to him I am now going.

The Duke, as I expected, was shaken to-day in his resolution of having himself named to the King. I say as I expected, for his brilliant imagination and ambitious energy easily catch fire at his first emotions, although he should betray no exterior symptoms except those of tranquillity. But the rein he has so long put upon his passions, which he has eternally had under command, and in which habit he has been most persevering, reconducts him to the hesitation of experience, and to that superabundant circumspection which his great diffidence of mankind, and his foible, I mean his dread of losing his reputation, incessantly inspire. He made a circumstantial display of the delicacy with which the petty glory, or, to speak plainly said he, the vain glory of the King must be managed.

Taking up the conversation at the point where we had left it, he assured me that, with respect to Welner, I was deceived; that he was one of the persons in Berlin on whom he depended, and who rather wished to see him in power than any other; that I might easily speak with him at the house of Moulinès (his resident, an artful man, but too ostensibly artful; ready to serve that he may better perform his office of spy, but proffering his services with too much facility; appointed to take part in the education of the Prince of Prussia, but hitherto without any title; a deserter from Prince Henry, since it has become pretty evident the Prince will never be in power; inclined to serve France, in general, and indeed too visibly, for he is styled the privy counsellor of Count d'Esterno, but in his heart solely attached to himself); that Welner goes there very often; that he certainly would not speak openly, at first, but that he would at length repeat whatever I should say, to the King.

The Duke often reiterated that he thought it useless and dangerous for him to be named; and, in fine, although with difficulty, and, as I may say, against his inclination, he gave me the true reason. In a fortnight he was to be at Berlin, or perhaps sooner; for (take particular notice of what follows) IT APPEARS THAT THE HOPE AFFORDED BY SIR JAMES HARRIS (the English ambassador at the Hague) OF A POWERFUL AND EFFICACIOUS SUCCOUR, SHOULD THE KING OF PRUSSIA RESOLVE, WITH AN ARMED FORCE, TO CREATE HIMSELF UMPIRE OF THE AFFAIRS OF HOLLAND, HAS INSPIRED THE KING WITH A WISH TO CONFER WITH HIS SERVANTS. I literally repeat the words the Duke pronounced, who fixed his eyes upon me, but whom I defy not only to have observed the least trait of emotion in my countenance, but still more not to have been struck with a smile, almost imperceptible and very ironical, as if I had known and contemned the fact. My only reply at the end of his sentence was, shrugging up my shoulders:—

"There is little need I should remark to you, my Lord, that the conquest which Louis XIV., Turenne, Condé, Luxembourg, Louvois, and two hundred thousand French, could not make of Holland, will never be effected by Prussia, watched by the Emperor, on that same country, now that it is supported by France."[1]

---

[1] Here it must be confessed the traveller was a false

The Duke therefore is going, or wishes to make us believe he is going, to Berlin; where deliberations are to be held on the propositions of England.

So be it. So much the better. Do not be alarmed. The Duke is rather German than Prussian, and as good a statesman as he is a great warrior. He will prove such a proposition to be so absurd that it is probably no more than the personal conception of the audacious and artful Harris, who wishes, at any expense, to make his fortune, and in a fit of madness to poniard his nation, which is more able than sage.

Still, however, I think my journey to Brunswick is a lucky accident; for I confess, and with great pleasure, I found the principles of the Duke to be moderate, prudent, and, politically speaking, wholly French. I depicted the affair, or rather affairs, as a whole, under new points of view; and if, as I persist in believing, or rather as I have believed more strongly, since I have known that he depends upon Welner for strengthening

---

prophet; but whether it was precisely his fault still remains to be enquired.

his party, his measures have long been taken (for Welner has been a canon at Halberstadt, where the regiment of the Duke remains), if I say, the necessity of accident should oblige him to take the helm, I shall have acquired the greatest advantages to treat with and make him a party in our designs.

He has desired I would give Count d'Esterno the very good advice, should Count Finckenstein die, or even should he not, to demand to treat on the affairs of Holland, and on all that relates to them, immediately with his Majesty. This is the most certain means of battering Hertzberg in breach, who certainly has been controverted with great firmness in these affairs by the King, and to obtain that which we shall seem only to expect from the judgment and personal will of the Monarch. It is a proceeding which is successful with all Kings, even with the greatest. Vanswieten obtained from Frederick II. himself the most important concessions, by acting thus; and this is certainly a much more safe, as it is a more noble mode, than all the deceitful efforts which flattery can employ with Prince Henry, whose glaring protection is more injurious to the French embassy than it ever can be productive of good, under the most favourable of future contingencies. For I am not very unapt to believe, as the Duke affirms without disguise, that this *partition Prince*,[1] were he master of affairs, would be the most dangerous of the enemies of Germanic freedom. I must conclude, for I have not time to cypher; the remainder of this inestimable conversation will be sent you hereafter. Inform me, with all possible expedition, how I ought to act under the present circumstances, and be persuaded that, if you can find any means whatever of giving me secret official credit with the King, or even with the Duke, you will act very wisely.

Additional Note.

If you do not imagine I am totally doting, mark me. I conjure you to read, and cause this to be read, with the utmost attention; and not

---

[1] *Ce Prince partageur :* alluding, no doubt, to the dismemberment of Poland, in which he was as *laudably* active as the just, the philosophic, the GREAT King, his brother, and from motives *equally pure*, as will be seen from the anecdote of the statue, related in the second volume.

to suffer me to wait a single moment for an answer, even though it should be absolutely necessary, for this purpose, to borrow some few hours from the levity of the country, or to be consistent for a whole day together.

LETTER XXXVIII

Berlin, October 21st, 1786.

I ARRIVED at half-past five in the morning. The King was to exercise his cavalry at six. I immediately mounted my horse, that I might discover the state of his health, observe what aspect he wore, and if possible to find some person to whom I might address myself. His health is good, his brow cloudy; the troops were obliged to wait a considerable time, and after two charges he very abruptly and very ridiculously retired. Nothing sufficiently new or important has come to my knowledge, to prevent my employing the few remaining moments, before the departure of the courier, and which are greatly abridged by your eight pages of cyphers, in resuming the consequences which I have drawn from the very interesting conversation, an account of which I gave you in my last despatch. It is impossible I should send you a complete and circumstantial narrative of all that passed, because that the Duke, an hour after I had left him, having sent me his minister for foreign affairs (M. von Ardensberg von Reventlau), I have too much to add.

Four particulars appeared to me evident.

I.—That, during the confidential conference with the Duke, a great complication of sensation, emotion, and design was mingled. He wishes we should aid him in becoming prime minister of Prussia; but that we should act with caution. He is not convinced that we desire to see him in that post (I did everything in my power to persuade him of it), yet perfectly satisfied that any interference in the affairs of Holland would be a stupid error, he is anxious that Prussia should act with propriety; and that, in this affair at least, we should acquire influence. He, therefore, while he informed me, endeavoured to discover if I already had any information, and whether we were determined in the pursuit of our projects. To the same purport were the after commentaries of Ardensberg, his deceptive confidences, and Gazette secrets; the recall not only of M. de Coetloury,[1] but also of M. de Veirac; our desertion of the

---

[1] I dare not positively affirm, but I am almost certain this name ought to be spelt Couette-Toury; and that the

patriotic party, &c., &c.—to all which particulars I replied with a smile.

II.—That the great inquietude of the Duke arises from not knowing whether we are or are not Austrians; or whether we are merely so undecided on the subject as that the errors, or the cold distance, of the Cabinet of Berlin will be sufficient to induce us, at the hazard of all that can happen, to second the Emperor in his designs against Germany. In my opinion, were the Duke freed from his apprehensions on this very capital article, he would be French; for he is strongly German, and the English can only set Germany in flames; we alone have the power of maintaining it in peace. Should his connections with England appear to be strengthened, it is but, as I think, because he distrusts the destiny of Prussia; for he well knows that his English calculations are rather specious than solid, and that the Prussian, though perhaps somewhat more subaltern, are much less hazardous.

---

person meant is the same who is mentioned in the second volume (during the conference between the author and Baron Reede) as the confidential friend of M. de Calonne.

III.—He and his minister have so often demanded, and redemanded, on what basis I imagined the pacification of Holland might be established, that I have supposed the Duke probably thinks, should we exclude the Prince of Prussia from the Nassau alliance, there might be a necessity of choosing his daughter, the Princess Caroline of Brunswick, as a consort for the Prussian heir. The supposition is founded on circumstances so fugitive that it is impossible to give them written evidence, or perhaps probable; especially because that, not having received any instructions on such a subject, I have not dared to make any advances. I therefore only give it for what it is worth. The being but little informed of the affairs of Holland has, in every respect, been highly injurious to me on this occasion. Might I have spoken more freely, I might even have drawn the well dry. The only positive proposal which he made on the subject was a kind of coalition-council of regency, without which the Stadtholder could effect nothing, and in which should be included Gislaer, Vanberckel, &c., &c.; but among whom also must be seated M. Van Lynden, the governor of the children of the Stadtholder, &c., &c. To my eternal objection—" How will you support those measures which shall be taken under the pledge of your aid ? "—he continually replied—" Should the Stadtholder counteract these arrangements, we will abandon him."—" But how far ? " I replied. " And, if but amicably, how will he be injured, should he be thus abandoned ? "——In a word, I continued, with a kind of mysterious obstinacy, to maintain that the Stadtholder would never be brought to reason, unless it should be declared to him that the King of Prussia would forsake his party; though his consort might be secretly informed such was not the real intent.

IV.—It appeared to me that the Duke was ruminating on some grand project for the reconstruction of the Germanic edifice; for this able Prince perceives the antique ruinous building must be propped in order to be preserved, and even in many parts repaired. The sole wish which he clearly testified was the separation of the electorate of Hanover from the English monarchy, and the secularisation of certain provinces, which might one day form an equivalent for Saxony. He supposes the first point might be gained, and even without any great difficulty, should our politics become anglicised; and that the second might be accomplished, though contrary to the confederation of the Princes, because at the death of the Elector of Mayence there will be an opportunity of retouching the league, as well as a natural and proper occasion of coming to an explanation with the ecclesiastical Princes, who, more interested than any others in the liberties of Germany, are always the first to tergiversate, &c., &c. Hence, we at least may learn that, however attached he may appear to be to the confederation, means may be found of inducing him to listen to reason concerning modifications.

The instructions which are necessary for me at present, are:—

I.—Whether we ought, on this occasion, to bring him on the stage, which would be the real means of driving him from it; and I certainly do not think the latter to be our interest, for he is more prudent, more able, and less susceptible of prejudice and passion, than any other who can be made minister.

II.—Whether his party ought to be encouraged and strengthened, which will be to act directly contrary to the party of Prince Henry; for the plan of the Duke is exclusive; and to confess the truth, he appears tacitly so convinced that the Prince can effect nothing, that he has greatly fortified my own opinion on this subject.

III.—What is the degree of confidence I ought to place in him? For it is impossible to obtain the confidence of, without placing confidence in, such a man; and in my apprehension he had better be told than suffer to divine.

Count Finckenstein is recovering.

The King arrived on the eighteenth, at eight in the morning, after having left Breslau, on the seventeenth, at seven in the morning. This was incredible diligence; no person could keep pace with him. He went on the same day to visit the Queen Dowager, and thus gave occasion to attribute the rapidity and danger of the journey to Mademoiselle Voss. She is said to be pregnant; but, in the first place this cannot be known, and, in the second, I do not believe the haste would have been so great, had it been truth. According to report, she has demanded two hundred thousand crowns. Should this be so, the circle of her career will not be very ample.

The King made a multitude of nobles in Silesia, as elsewhere. But, without loading my letter, the Gazettes will tell you enough of their names. He is to remain a week at Potsdam, which is to be dedicated to his military labours. Great changes in the army are spoken of, such as will be favourable to the subalterns, and the reverse to the captains.

The Dantzicers, who, according to appearances, supposed Kings were hobgoblins, were so enraptured to meet with one who did not eat their children that, in the excess of their enthusiasm, they were willing to put themselves without restraint under the Prussian government. The magistrates eluded the folly of the populace as well as they could, under the pretence that Dantzic was dependent on Poland; but so great and so violent was the tumult, that Prussian and Polish couriers were sent off. This event will no doubt rouse the Emperor and Russia; a favourable circumstance to our affairs in Holland.

Count Hertzberg, who has indulged himself in very headlong acts in Silesia, and particularly in his discourse on the day of homage, in which he really braved the Emperor in a very indecent manner, as if it was not in his nature to accommodate himself to a peaceable order of affairs; Hertzberg, I say, has had the influence to retard the nomination of Alvensleben for the French Embassy, which had been announced by the King at supper. How might I have expected to be thus deceived, since, when I sent you the intelligence, I supposed it to be an affair so public that I did not even write it in cypher?

LETTER XXXIX

October 24th, 1786.

I SHALL begin my despatch with an anecdote, the truth of which is undoubted, and which appears to me the most decisive of all I have learnt concerning the new reign. Recollect that, in Number XVIII., August 29, I wrote,

"The King apparently intends to renounce all his old habits. This is a proud undertaking. He retires before ten in the evening, and rises at four. Should he persevere, he will afford a singular example of habits of thirty years being vanquished. This will be an indubitable proof of a grand character, and shew how we have all been mistaken."

When I spoke thus, I, like the rest of the world, judged by appearances. The truth is that at half after nine the King disappeared, and was supposed to be gone to rest; whereas, in the most retired apartments of the palace, like another Sardanapalus, he held his orgies till night was far advanced. Hence it is easy to understand why hours of business were obliged to be inverted. Health would not allow him to be equally active upon the stage and behind the scenes.

Prince Henry regards himself as kept at a distance as well from system as from inclination. He is, or believes himself to be, persuaded that the innumerable follies which will result from his absence, for in his opinion the country without his aid is undone, will occasion recourse to be had to his experience and his abilities, and he then intends to refuse that tardy succour which his genius will be implored to yield. Even granting him the truth of all these vain dreams, he does not recollect that the expression of an undone country is only true relative to a certain lapse of time, and that therefore, in all probability, he will be dead before the want of his assistance will be perceived. He comes to reside four months at Berlin; there, according to him, to suffer martyrdom, that it may not be supposed he has deserted the public cause. His places of asylum are afterward to be Rheinsberg, the Lake of Geneva, and France; but such he will easily find everywhere. Consolation will not be wanting to him, since consolation can be found at playing at blind man's-buff, or hot-cockles, with actresses more insipid than the very worst of our provincial companies can afford.

The distribution of influence continues the same. Hertzberg violently seizes on the King, who probably has more esteem for Count Finckenstein; but whom, not being so eternally hunted by him, he leaves in a subaltern degree of credit, which from apparent may become real, the easy temper of the master considered. The remaining ministers are held to be so many cyphers.

Welner daily increases his jurisdiction, and Bishopswerder his influence, but he does not appear to exercise this influence either as a man of ostentation or a dupe. He neither asks for titles, ribands, nor places. At most he will but make ministers; he will never be one. Three hundred thousand livres (twelve thousand five hundred pounds sterling) for each of his daughters, an excellent fief for himself, with military rank (he is said to be a good officer)—these are what he wishes, and these he most probably *will* obtain. In the meantime no person *has* anything; neither he nor Welner nor Goertz, who lives by borrowing.

Bowlet?—The influence of a mason-engineer, and no other; for of no other is he capable.

Goltz the Tartar?—Artful, sly, dexterous; perhaps ambitious, but very selfish and covetous. Money is his ruling passion, and money he will have. He will probably have the greatest influence over military affairs, unless the Duke of Brunswick should take them to himself. The memorials relative to fortification are transmitted to him.

Colonel Wartensleben is evidently kept at a distance, and probably because of his family connexions with Prince Henry; who, to all his other disadvantages, adds that of having every person who is about the King for his enemy.

Subalterns?—Their kingdom is not come. It should seem that having long, while Prince of Prussia, been deceived by them, the King knows and recollects this; although from compassion he wishes not to notice it, at least for a time.

The master?—What is he?—I persist in believing it would be rash, at present, to pronounce, though one might be strongly tempted to reply *King Log*. No understanding, no fortitude, no consistency, no industry; in his pleasures the Hog of Epicurus[1] and the hero only of pride; which perhaps we should rather denominate confined and vulgar vanity. Such hitherto have the symptoms been. And under what circumstances, in what an age, and at what a post? I am obliged to summon all my reason to divine, and to forget it all again to hope. The thing which is really to be feared is lest the universal contempt he must soon incur should irritate him, and deprive him of that species of benevolence of which he shews signs. That weakness is very formidable which unites an ardent thirst after pleasures, destitute of choice or delicacy, with the desire of keeping them secret in a situation where nothing can be kept secret.

Not that I here am writing a second part to Madam de Sévigné; I do not speak ill of Frederick-William because he overlooks me, as she spoke well of Louis XIV., because he had lately danced a minuet with her.

---

[1] *Epicuri de grege porcum.*—Hor.

Yesterday, at the Court of the Queen, he three times addressed himself to me, which he never before did in public.—" You have been at Magdeburg and Brunswick."—"Yes, Sire."—"Were you pleased with the manœuvres?"—" Sire, I was in admiration."—" I ask to be informed of the truth, and not to be complimented."—" In my opinion, Sire, there was nothing wanting to complete the splendour of this exhibition, except the presence of your Majesty."—" Is the Duke in good health?"—" Exceedingly good, Sire."—"Will he be here soon?"—" Your Majesty, I imagine, is the only person who knows."—He smiled.

This is a specimen. You will well imagine it was, personally, very indifferent to me what he should say to me before the whole Court, but it was not so to the audience; and I note this as having appeared to make a part of the arranged reparation to France, which reparation was as follows. (From this, imagine the wit of the Court of Berlin; for I am convinced there was a real desire of giving satisfaction to Count d'Esterno.)

First it was determined the Queen should have a Lotto, and not a private party, in order that the company at her table might be the more numerous. After all the Princesses, Prince Henry, Prince Frederick of Brunswick, and the Prince of Holsteinbeck, had been invited, and taken their places, Mademoiselle Bishopswerder, the maid of honour who regulated the party, named Count d'Esterno. The Queen then, perceiving Lord Dalrymple, beckoned him, and at the same moment desired him to sit down. The ambassadors of France and England were the only foreign ministers that were of the party, so that Princes Reuss and Romanzow were now excluded, as they before had appeared to have been favoured. It would be difficult to imagine anything more awkward, or more inconsistent; and this increases my regret at remembering that Count d'Esterno thought himself obliged to take offence on the first Court day of the Queen; for, after the absurdity of yesterday, I can see no possible hope of reparation, which would not be slovenly daubing.

I am certain, however, that, far from wishing to wound, they were desirous to heal; and, to treat the subject less petitely, I am persuaded it is wrong to affirm the King hates the French. He hates nothing; he scarcely *loves* anything. He has been told that he must become wholly German, in order to pursue a new and glorious track, and he descends to the level of his nation, instead of desiring to elevate his nation superior to itself. His conduct is the result of the narrowness of his views. If he have a cordial dislike to anything, it is to men of wit; because he imagines that, in their company, it is absolutely requisite he should hear wit, and be himself a wit. He despairs of the one, and therefore hates the other. He has not yet learnt that men of wit only are the people who can appear not to possess wit. He seems to have made a determination to treat all persons in an amicable manner, without haughtiness or threat. The Stadtholder always receives two very different accounts from Berlin, and does not fail to believe that which flatters his ruling passion.

A mile from this place some very secret experiments are making on the artillery, which are confided to Major Tempelhoff. A small number of superior officers are admitted; captains are excluded. The ground is covered by tents, and guarded by sentinels, night and day. I shall endeavour to learn the particulars.

I forgot to write you word, from Brunswick, that the Duchess informed me the Prince of Wales was consulting the most able civilians in Europe, to learn whether, by marrying a Catholic, the positive laws of England, the laws of any other nation, or the maxims of the civil laws of Europe, would disinherit an heir, and particularly an Heir-Apparent. There appears to be much imprudence in this appeal of an Heir-Apparent from the opinions of Great Britain to those of the civilians.[1]

An anecdote less important, but perhaps more poignant, is that the Margrave of Baden-Baden has sent M. von Edelsheim here as his complimentary envoy, the brother of one of his ministers who is called the Choiseul of Carlsruhe. The following is

---

[1] The political conduct of the Prince appears to rise with, and become equal to, political exigencies. There are strong symptoms in his late behaviour of a fortitude that is equal to the glorious heroism of despising *self* when self and the welfare of mankind are at warfare. Love, the crimes of which, if so crimes can be, are venial, has yielded to a less seductive, but more noble passion.

the history of this complimentor, who has arrived long after all the others.

At a time when the prolific virtues of the father of the five royal children were held in doubt, there was a wish to bestow a lover on a lady (the afterwards divorced Queen, banished to Stettin), who, had they not done so, would have made bold to have bestowed one on herself. The care of choosing was committed to the brothers of the Duke of Brunswick. They descended a little too low, and in consequence an eye was cast on Edelsheim, who was publicly enough charged with this great work. He was afterwards sent to Paris to execute another commission,[1] of which

---

[1] Frederick II., dreading the tediousness of the proposed congress at Augsburg, wished to send a private emissary to sound the Court of France. For this purpose he chose Edelsheim as a person, according to the King's account, least liable to suspicion. The project of Frederick was to indemnify the King of Poland by robbing the ecclesiastical Princes of Germany. This the pious Louis XV. rejected. Edelsheim returned with his answer to Frederick at Freyberg, whence he afterwards departed for London, made his communications, and was once again sent back to Paris, on pretence that he had left some of his travelling trunks there; and the Bailli de Froulay, the ambassador of the Knights of Malta, being persuaded the French were effec-

he acquitted himself ill. I have been assured he was thrown into the Bastille. On his return he was disgraced, but afterwards employed, and sent to various Courts of Germany in 1778. And this is the man whom, in his high wisdom, the Margrave selected for his envoy to the King of Prussia. The Monarch himself, when he saw him, could not forbear laughing.

Postscript.—Yesterday, at eleven in the morning, the King, hid in a grey coach, went alone to Mon-Bijou, where he remained an hour, whence he returned in a great glow. What does this mean? Is this the triumph of the lady Voss? It is impossible at present to know. Neither has anything transpired concerning the letters which M. von Calenberg has brought from the Stadtholder.

Muller and Landsberg, private secretaries of the Cabinet, demanded their dismission with

---

tually desirous of peace, was, as he had been before, the mediator. The Bailli was deceived. The Duke de Choiseul, indecently enough, threw Edelsheim into the Bastille in order to search his papers, which, however, Edelsheim had taken care to secure. The emissary was released on the morrow, but obliged to depart the kingdom, by the way of Turin. Such is the story as related by the King, in Chapter XI. of the Seven Years' War.

considerable chagrin; their services not being apparently necessary, said they, since they were not thought worthy of being instructed concerning the answers they had to return, and since the letters were sent ready composed to the King. They remain in their places, and the accommodation was effected by Bishopswerder. It appears that he is in league with Welner against Hertzberg, which he does not take any great precautions to conceal. The King will not go to Potsdam to make the military arrangements before Friday, in order, as it is supposed, to give the Duke time to arrive. The attempting to account for all the caprices of Kings is a strange kind of frenzy.

LETTER XL.

October 28th, 1786.

I PASSED yesterday evening with Prince Henry. The King had dedicated almost the whole afternoon of the day before to this palace; for, after having been with the Prince, he visited the Princess, where he played, and drank tea with Mademoiselle Voss, among other ladies of honour. This kind of reconciliation with the Prince (which, however, is nothing more than a simple act of courtesy, as is evident from the succeeding visit to the Princess, whom the Prince regards as his most cruel enemy), this reconciliation (which is nearly an accurate phrase; for the coolness between them was very great) appears to be the political work of Welner, who wishes, in his struggle against Hertzberg, if not the support, at least the neutrality of the Prince; and the hatred of this feeble mortal is so blind in effect that, united with the hopes of his ambition, of which he is not easy to be cured, it was sufficient to induce him once more meanly to offer his services to the King; consequently to cast himself, if possible, to a greater distance. Not that he himself places any great dependence on this type of peace, which is the more suspicious because it happened on the eve of a succeeding fortnight's absence, after which it will not be difficult to find pretences not to meet again for some time longer, should the King think proper. But the Prince imagines his enemy dead, and he enjoys himself, and chuckles like a child, without recollecting that this is the very way to promote his resurrection.

In reality Count Hertzberg appears to have cast his own die. He had a tolerable run of ill-luck in Silesia: abrupt disputes, contradictions, the chagrin of seeing the name of the brother of his former mistress struck off from the list of Counts; he ought, even while in Prussia, to have perceived that his sounding speeches gave no pleasure. On the day of receiving homage, he read over the names of the Counts, and when he came to his own stopped, that the King, seated on his throne, might pronounce it himself; and the Monarch was malicious enough to remain silent, so that the inauguration of Count Hertzberg did not take place till the day after, and in the ante-chamber.

But what probably has occasioned his downfall, if fallen he has, was his haughty behaviour to Welner, the least forgetful of men, and who, amid his ambitious projects, needed no such cause of rancour to occasion him to hate and injure the minister. Hertzberg has made him wait for hours in his ante-chamber, has received and kept him standing, spoken to him but a very short time, and dismissed him with airs which are only proper to give offence. Welner vowed his destruction, and he is seconded by Bishopswerder.

Such, at least, are probabilities, according to every acceptation of the word influence; and I should have divined them to-day from the very politeness of Hertzberg. He gave a grand dinner to foreigners, among whom for once Count d'Esterno and myself were invited. His attention seemed all directed to us. Such proceedings are awkward and mean. This mixture of stiffness and twining is a strange singularity by which half-formed characters ruin themselves. Machiavel rightly affirms that "all the evil in the world originates in not being sufficiently good, or sufficiently wicked." Whether my conjectures are or are not true, still it is certain Count Hertzberg has been very dryly and positively forbidden all interference, direct or indirect, in the affairs of Holland, from which country Callenberg does not appear to have brought any remarkable intelligence. He is really come to obtain admission into the Prussian service, and his letters were only recommendatory.

It is not the influence of Hertzberg that prevents the recall of Thulemeyer, but that of Count Finckenstein. The mother of the envoy has had a lasting and tender friendship for the Count; and indeed it was her husband who procured the Count a place in the ministry. In fact, it appears to me to be a matter of little moment, for the present, whether Thulemeyer should or should not be recalled. His embassy ended on the arrival of Goertz, nor do I believe he sends any despatches.

The destiny of Launay was decided the day

before yesterday by a very severe letter. He is
no longer allowed to act, and they only offer him
a pension of two thousand crowns to retire on,
with the proviso that he shall remain in the
Prussian states. It must be owned his estimate[1]
is a chef-d'œuvre of egotism and folly, and that
he might be completely refuted; although the
memorial of the commissioners who have undertaken his refutation is a pitiable performance. He
has proved two facts, the one of which is curious,
and the other decisive against his own administration. First, that, in the space of nineteen
years, he has brought into the King's coffers a
surplus of forty-two millions six hundred and
eighty-nine thousand crowns of the empire (or
upward of seven millions sterling) exclusive of the
fixed revenue, which annually amounted to five
millions of crowns. What dreadful oppression!—
The second, that the collecting of the customs is
an annual expense of more than one million four
hundred thousand crowns (or near two hundred
and fifty thousand pounds sterling), which, on a
first view of the business to be transacted, and

---

[1] Compte rendu.

of local circumstances, might at least be reduced two-thirds. But not one man is at this moment employed who appears to understand the elements of his profession. It is a fact that they have not yet been able to make any general statement of debtor and creditor, nor to class any single branch of the revenue; so that there is not one object, not even the King's dinner, which is yet regulated.

This is a chaos, but it is a chaos at rest. Finance, military and civil, are each alike in a state of stagnation; and such a state in general would indeed be better than the rage of governing too much, in a country with a fixed constitution, in which individual prudence might preponderate over public folly. But men are here so accustomed to see their King active, or rather exclusively active; they are so little in the habit of doing what he leaves undone; though, having once issued his orders, they very well understand the art of deceiving him; they even think so little of laying any proposals before him, that the stagnation is a real clog on the machine. But how injurious may this clog become in a kingdom which rests on so brittle a basis, though inhabited, indeed, by a people so tardy, so heavy, so unimpassioned, that it is scarcely possible a sudden shock should happen? The vessel, however, must continue to sink, more or less sensibly, if some pilot does not come on board, although she will not suddenly founder.

Wait we must: it would be an act of temerity to attempt to look into this darkness visible. I repeat we must wait before we can know whether the King will, or will not, have the courage to take a prime minister. Such an appointment would be equal to a revolution; and, well or ill, would change the whole face of affairs.

The Duke of Brunswick is the person who ought to be narrowly watched, if we wish to foretell the fate of this Government; although he should not be the person appointed, and should there be any appearance of a shipwreck. This Prince is only fifty, and is indisputably ambitious. Should he ever resolve on hazardous and daring designs, and should he no longer depend on Prussia, he would shake all the German combinations as the north wind shakes the reed. His manners and his prudence are incompatible with the English party. Neither can England act on the Continent except accidentally. But I can imagine circumstances under which I think him capable of going over to the Emperor, who would receive him with open arms. And what might not the Duke of Brunswick perform at the head of the Austrian army? How great would be the danger of Germany! How vast a prospect for him whose passions might be unbridled, should he be obliged to act a desperate part; for he almost hates his sons, unless it be his youngest, who promises not to be so stupid as the others.

      ✧   ✧   ✧   ✧   ✧

The best manner of securing him has been missed, which would have been to have placed him unconditionally at the head of the Germanic Confederation. Should he desert it, I greatly fear he will be its destroyer.

Baron H—— is arrived, and has not been received by the King equal to his expectations. A certain musical demoniac, named Baron Bagge, is also at Berlin.[1] I imagine they are all in too

---

[1] This Baron is a very pleasant gentleman, at least to the musical world. He performs on the violin, but so

much haste. The King is in the high fervour of the German system, and anxious to have it known that the ship is to be differently trimmed. Since his accession, the banker of La Valmour has received orders to send in his account, that it may be discharged, and to stop all future payments to that girl who had formerly so much power over him. It is said he is to return from Potsdam on the third, and I imagine it will be found that he only goes there to the chase. The Prince of Dessau is to arrive there to-morrow evening, and I have no doubt there is to be a calling of the faithful.[1]

---

vilely, and with such ridiculous vanity, that there is not a great city in Europe in which he is not mimicked by the musicians; who, however, take good care to flatter him, and to serve whom he devotes his time and his income. His usual residence is at Paris, where he keeps open house for all who can hold a fiddle, and does not scruple, there and elsewhere, to invite the men who have gained most reputation in the practice of their art to take lessons of him and acquire absolute perfection.

[1] *Evocation d'âmes.*

LETTER XLI

October 30th, 1786.

At the request of Struensee, I have sent him the following information. First on the possibility of public loans to France, and secondly on the treaty of commerce, and on the manner of placing money in the French funds.

There are two species of public funds in France; those the interest of which is fixed and certain, and which does not vary with circumstances; and those which produce dividends, or a participation of gain, subject to vicissitudes and to rise or fall.

The public and favoured companies principally appertain to this last class. Such as the Caisse d'Escompte, the Paris water-works, and French East India Company; the prices of stock in which have successively, or all together, been agitated by every frenzy of stock-jobbing. All true estimate of their real value and their effective gains has been as it were lost, that men might yield to the rage of gambling in funds which never could be reduced to any exact valuation. These jobbers have been less occupied by endeavours to reduce the price of shares to their true value than artfully to affect their price, by disputes and pretended reasonings on the impossibility of delivering all the shares that had been sold. Monopoly has succeeded to monopoly, association to association; some to raise, others to lower the price; to effect which every imaginary species of deceit, cabal, and cunning has been practised; and, though this gambling mania has not continued more than two years, many people have already been ruined, and many others dishonoured, by taking shelter under the laws to elude their engagements.

The other species of public funds, and the only one perhaps which merits the name, consists in contracts, and royal effects, properly so called. The contracts yield an interest of from five and a half to six per cent. at the utmost. One only fund, the stock of which is paid at sight, is more productive. This is the loan of one hundred and twenty-five millions. Shares are only sold, at present, at an advance of two per cent., although there are nine months' interest due, and that the real interest amounts to nearly seven per cent. The stock cannot remain long at this price; and, whether the purchasers wish to be permanent stock-holders, or only to speculate for some months, this loan merits a preference to any other. Its advantages annually increase, since, while receiving a uniform interest of five per cent., a part of the capital is to be periodically repaid. In January, 1787 and 1788, these reimbursements are to be made at the rate of fifteen per cent. on the capital advanced. They are afterwards to proceed to pay off twenty per cent., and at intervals of three years to twenty-five, thirty, thirty-five, forty, forty-five, fifty per cent ; till, in the last year, the whole will be repaid, independent of the interest of five per cent. to, and including, the years of reimbursement, the last year of payment only excepted. The stock-holders may either have bills payable at sight, according to the original plan, or if they please may receive contracts in their stead, without any change taking place in the order of reimbursement.

Those who buy in with a design of remaining

stock-holders must prefer contracts, because these are neither liable to be stolen, burnt, nor destroyed. Those who purchase stock on speculation, intending to sell out, should rather receive bills, because the transfer would then be subject to none of the delays of office.

We ought to regard the public loans of France as at an end, all the debts of the war being paid; so that, if any loans henceforth should take place, they can probably be only for small sums[1] to pay off the annual reimbursements with which the finances will, for five or six years to come, be burdened. But these loans can only offer trifling advantages to the moneyed men. The rate of interest must have a natural tendency to fall, because of the general prosperity of the kingdom, and consequently the loan of one hundred and twenty-five millions presents the probability of rising in price; which rise is each day liable to take place, and which variation cannot be profited by, unless stock is immediately purchased. This probability might even be called a certainty, when

---

[1] The world at that time was ignorant of, nor could it divine, the sublime invention of gradual and successive loans.

on the one part we recollect the nature of the loan, which is the most wise, solid, and advantageous to the moneyed men, and in every respect the best that has ever been imagined; and on the other the concurrence of circumstances, which all uniting lead us to presume that the credit of France, and the public confidence in its royal effects, must daily increase.

On the Commercial Treaty.

It appears that the Treaty of Commerce is highly acceptable to both parties. The English perceive in it a vast market for their woollen cloths, wrought cottons, and hardware; we depend on the great exportation of our wines, linens, and cambrics; and probably both nations are right, but under certain modifications, the value of which can only be taught by time.

The treaty, in general, seems to have held a principle as sacred which has too often been misunderstood; which is, that moderate duties are the sole means of preserving the revenue, and preventing illicit trade. Thus the English merchandise is rated at from ten to twelve per cent.

Should the advantage for some years appear to be wholly on the side of the English, still it is evident the French trade will gain ground, since nothing can prevent our manufactures gradually imitating the products of English industry; whereas, Nature having refused soil and climate to England, our wines cannot be made there, and in this respect the English must always depend on us.

True it is that the wines of Portugal will continue to be drank in England in great quantities, but the rising generation will prefer the wines of France. Of this Ireland affords a proof, in which ten times the quantities of French wines are drank to the wines of Portugal. The French wines henceforth are only to pay duties equivalent to those which the wines of Portugal at present pay in England; that is to say, forty pounds sterling per ton, or about one shilling per bottle. Our wines of Medoc may there be sold cheap, and will be preferred to the wines of Portugal. The English, it is true, are allowed to lower the present duties on the wines of Portugal, but they will fear to diminish them too sensibly, lest they should injure the revenue arising from their beer, which is the most essential of their excise duties, and annually produces more than one million eight hundred thousand pounds sterling.

The treaty, in fact, will incontestably be advantageous to both countries. It will procure an increase of enjoyment to the people, and of revenue to their respective Monarchs. Its tendency is to render the English and French more friendly, and in general it is founded on those liberal principles which are worthy two such great nations, and of which France ought to be the first to give an example, since, of all countries on earth, it would, from its natural advantages, be the greatest gainer, should such principles be universally established in the commercial world.

LETTER XLII

October 31st, 1786.

*   *   *

They have also affirmed (that is, Prince Ferdinand has) that it was I who refuted the estimate[1] of Launay. From that moment I have daily left my card at the house of Launay, and have declared that to torment people seemed to me to be a thing so unnecessary that, exclusive of the cowardice of wantonly striking a man under misfortunes, none but a fool could have invented so silly and malicious a tale.

On the reply to the refutation of his estimate, Launay received so severe a letter that he immediately demanded permission to retire. The King answered this should be granted him, when the commission should have no more need of his assistance.

It is loudly rumoured here, after having been long whispered, that a treaty is concerting between Russia, Austria, and Prussia; the pretext for which is the pacification of Holland. I own

---
[1] Compte rendu.

that at present I do not see the least probability of truth in the report. Neither the King, nor any of his ministers, appear to me to have an understanding sufficiently enlarged for such a project. Not but we most assuredly ought to pay very serious attention to the rumour.

As I was finishing my phrase, I received information that Doctor Roggerson, the favourite physician of the Czarina, the same whom she sent to Vienna, and of whom I spoke to you in my former despatches, is just arrived. Now or never is the time for an *eye war;* but this kind of tilting can be performed only by ambassadors; they alone possess the means, were we to exclude every other except the all-puissance of supper parties, which are the very sieves of secrets.

Roggerson returns from England by way of Amsterdam, and Berlin was entirely in his road. Still, I repeat, we ought watchfully to observe Vienna and Petersburg; convinced as I am at present that the Emperor is only spreading nets for this country. I must further add that I imagine I very clearly perceive the Gallomania of Prince Henry is on the decline. But this to him will be of no advantage, for it is to oppose the Prince that they are Anti-Gallican here. It is not to oppose the French that he is opposed. Prince Henry is turbulent, false, and perfidious. He formerly was successful at Petersburg. He may flatter himself that, should there be any need of that Court, he may be employed; and never will there be a better resemblance of the morality of the late Erostratus.[1]

The Duke of Brunswick arrived on Saturday at Potsdam. This is a kind of secret at Berlin. Nothing had been done on Sunday, except listening to music and looking at reviews; but two couriers were certainly sent off, from the Sunday to the Tuesday. I know nothing more. I am in want of pecuniary and other aid. The domestic disorder is a thing so inconvenient, some of the favourites are so interested to put an end to it, or to certain parts of it, since they have not a sixpence, and it is carried to such excess in the palace, that I cannot help supposing there

---
[1] Meaning the late King, who fired not only temples, but would have willingly extended the conflagration to the universe, could he have thrown on the oil without being scorched by the gust of the flames.

is some grand object which employs the whole attention of the King, and the few moments he can prevail on himself to dedicate to business.

There has been a quarrel in the household, in which the master has committed some violence on himself. One of his favourite ushers, Rumpel, a man naturally very insolent, insomuch that at a review he once struck a gentleman without any serious notice being taken of the affair, has had a very passionate brawl with Lindenau, the new first usher, who is a Saxon, and the friend of Bishopswerder, who procured him the place. Lindenau put the insolent favourite under arrest, and gave an account of his proceeding to the King. The Monarch started with astonishment; but, after a momentary silence, he not only approved of the act of Lindenau, but confirmed the arrest in a very cool manner, and for an indefinite term. By this he has given some energy to the head servants, and somewhat tempered the insolence of the subalterns.

Discord, on the other hand, reigns among the favourites. Goltz and Bishopswerder had a very serious dispute in Silesia. The King, having made some new appointments, in favour of I know not whom, Goltz kept so cool a silence that the King insisted on knowing the reason of this tacit disapprobation. Goltz replied, "Your Majesty is overflowing the land with Saxons, as if you had not a subject of your own."—Bishopswerder came in, a few moments afterwards, and proposed another Saxon, on which the King very abruptly exclaimed, "Zounds! you never propose anybody but Saxons."—Probably, in the explanation which succeeded this pettishness, the King told what Goltz had said. Certain it is that Bishopswerder and Goltz have been very warm. The wall is whitewashed over, but we may with good reason conclude that Goltz, the Tartar, and Bishopswerder, the débonnaire, neither do, nor ever will, cordially esteem each other. It was the latter who brought the insignificant Duke of Holsteinbeck hither, and who is endeavouring to advance him to the command of the guards, that he may deprive the former favourite, Wartensleben, of the place.

To descend a step lower, it appears that Chauvier is regaining credit. He imagined, at the beginning of the reign, that the surliness of the secretary would promote his interest. It did the reverse. Apparently he has altered his route, and is in the pandar department, submits to subaltern complaisance, and even to act the spy, in which he finds his account.

The King returns on Wednesday, as it is said, to depart again on Thursday. I cannot understand what this means, unless it should be to keep Prince Henry at a distance, without openly quarrelling. The Prince will remain ignorant of affairs by not knowing where to find the King. The minister, Blumenthal, has rather resolutely demanded his dismission, complaining that His Majesty, having bedizened some of his servants, who were not of so long a standing as himself, with ribands, had not bestowed on him that mark of honour. His retreat, which is not granted, is a matter of little moment; though it is affirmed the King could not be better pleased, for he would then have a place to bestow. I have heard, and from a good quarter, that this place, or rather a place of principal trust, will very soon be given to a remarkable man, to the dissatisfaction of everybody. I can neither divine who this man is, nor believe the King has the fortitude to dissatisfy everybody. The credit of Hertzberg, if not ruined, is still on the decline. It is certain that he has not dined with the King since the return from Silesia.

Welner is at Potsdam.

Do not suffer your ambassador to persuade you that there is nothing to apprehend from Austria; I am convinced the King is undetermined, that the Emperor is sounding him, and that there is something in agitation with which we are unacquainted. For my own part, nothing would appear less extraordinary to me. I own I am surprised at all the intelligence I obtain, however little that all may be. But nothing can here be kept secret from a French ambassador, who is neither in want of money nor industry.

I have just been told that General Rodig has sent a challenge to Count Goertz. I have not learnt what was the cause of quarrel, and the truth of the news scarcely appears to be probable; yet it comes from a person who should know, though he is a young man.

END OF VOL. I

www.ingramcontent.com/pod-product-compliance
Lightning Source LLC
Chambersburg PA
CBHW030305240426
43673CB00040B/1073